Aberdeenshire
COUNCIL

Aberdeenshire Libraries
www.aberdeenshire.gov.uk/libraries

How to Be an
Overnight Success

How to Be an Overnight Success

Maria Hatzistefanis

1 3 5 7 9 10 8 6 4 2

Ebury Press, an imprint of Ebury Publishing,
20 Vauxhall Bridge Road,
London SW1V 2SA

Ebury Press is part of the Penguin Random House group
of companies whose addresses can be found
at global.penguinrandomhouse.com

Copyright © Maria Hatzistefanis 2017

First published by Ebury Press in 2017

www.eburypublishing.co.uk

A CIP catalogue record for this book is available from
the British Library

ISBN 9781785037320

Typeset in India by Integra Software Services Pvt. Ltd, Pondicherry

Printed and bound in Great Britain by Clays Ltd, St Ives PLC

Penguin Random House is committed to a
sustainable future for our business, our readers
and our planet. This book is made from Forest
Stewardship Council® certified paper.

To Stratis, Aris & Aki

Contents

Introduction: How I Became an Overnight Success

I always thought it was meant to be calm at the centre of a whirlwind. Well, I'm at the centre and this is definitely not calm. My phone has not stopped ringing. If it isn't another TV or magazine interview, it's another order, or someone at the office, or a celebrity publicist asking for products to Ellie Goulding and Jourdan Dunn. I am juggling phone, bags, product samples and a coffee as I attempt to get a cab to Heathrow to fly to New York for, yes … another TV interview, another deal and a product launch. The cause of this storm is my revolutionary product, Snake Serum, by my suddenly quite famous company Rodial.

The word is out and everyone is asking, 'How did you become an overnight success?'

I wasn't expecting this. Well, let's be clear, I am loving it, and I was hoping for it … I just wasn't expecting it! *Vogue* magazine is asking for a quote – it's doing a piece about the celebrity fans of the product, the waiting lists and sell-outs. (NB: If you want a sell-out, tell people it's selling out!) The German distributors we've been in talks with for a while have suddenly decided they need me to fly to Germany as they need the contract for our magic serum signed right now and, by the way, can they place an order for tens of thousands of units? A TV channel in Europe has just picked up the story and it is doing a live 'before and after' demo on camera to show the instant anti-ageing results. Elsewhere in Europe, a major retailer has put the product in 200 of its stores; at the cash point they are merchandising the theme with rubber snakes. Love it. At the airport, I pick up the *Sunday Times* and I'm on the front page, and there's a full-page feature on how I made it ... and how I'm an overnight success. It is non-stop. I turn my phone off as the plane doors close. At last a moment of calm and it occurs to me that I'm not AT the centre of this storm, I AM the centre ... so actually, the legend holds true. It is calm, because I am calm. This is wonderful. This is why I started this business.

Meanwhile, back home in the UK, the product is flying off the shelves at Harrods, Harvey Nichols and Space NK, and it's the same story in the US at Saks Fifth Avenue. This means I need to get on the line to our factories to approve them working overtime, weekends and evenings to fill the orders and make as much product as possible to cope with this unprecedented demand. I need more phones ... or ears, or both ... because now more publicists and agents are calling in our miraculous products for their celebrity clients and I'm hearing from the office that we are inundated with calls to get the product in goodie bags at VIP events. I am co-hosting a dinner with Poppy Delevingne and, on my way, I stop by Central Saint Martins College to speak to the students about a new project. Oh wait, do I have time to fit in an Instagram post on my @mrsrodial account in between? Make it quick as the phone is ringing ... can I fly to NY to film *Project Runway* for my mentoring episode next week?

And it just gets better. To front our campaigns, I'm working with Erin O'Connor, Daisy Lowe and Kylie Jenner. I count designers Mary Katrantzou, David Koma and Henry Holland as my friends. I'm travelling the world for press events and to speak at conferences in London, NY, LA and Tokyo.

My name is Maria Hatzistefanis (aka @mrsrodial – my alter ego) and I am the Founder and CEO of The Rodial Group, comprising two mega brands, Rodial and NIP+FAB. The combined two brands are available in over 20,000 stores and 35 countries worldwide.

So, how did I become an Overnight Success?

We are in 2017. I started the business in 1999. It took me 18 years to become an overnight success.

OK … but surely some actual overnight success stories do exist: I mean, iPod just came out of nowhere and changed the MP3-player market overnight, right? And Twitter changed the face of social media out of the blue? And you remember when Angry Birds came out of nowhere and suddenly everyone was playing it? Well, not quite.

The iPod launched in 2001 but it wasn't that well received. It wasn't until the fourth version that came out in 2004 that if finally took off. Biz Stone, founder of Twitter, had been trying to launch various blogging and mobile products for eight years before he found the right formula. And Rovio, the company behind Angry Birds, had been through 50 games and was on the verge of bankruptcy when Angry Birds hit. The exception to the rule is probably YouTube. But even though it was a virtual overnight success, it took five years to make a profit! I have yet to find a brand that was created overnight and had a sustainable business model. Overnight success is really just overnight exposure.

And to get your business that exposure, you are going to have to keep on pushing. There will be days you look around at other businesses and think: 'Why aren't I getting that publicity?' Or 'Why am I not selling out in my stores? What's wrong with me? I might as well just give up.' Just remember, it's not a race. You have to get it right, so when you do become an 'overnight success' you are ready for it. It's all about being consistent with your message and product and knowing who your customer and your brand are. Be consistent, deliver the same message on your product, your media, your digital presence so that people can recognise and remember you and your brand. It takes years to make an overnight success. And once you are there you have to keep challenging yourself. Do not stand still, do not stagnate. As an entrepreneur, you never reach a point where you say, I am very successful now, I achieved all the success I ever wanted. You need to progress your business, grow it, reinvent it and find new, exciting products and services to launch.

I want to share my story with you of how I made it to where I am right now. I didn't always know what I wanted to be, I changed career three times before I started my own business and I was fired from my last job. I have made a lot of mistakes, taken a lot of risks and found small and some bigger successes along the way. I always turn to stories of strong successful women and I am inspired by their journeys, and I would like to do the exact same thing for you. Inspire you, show you the way and share with you how I overcame obstacles and challenges while keeping my eye on the ball. I want to motivate you to pursue your dreams and keep on going even if everything is against you, and to teach you to believe in yourself even if no one else will.

I can't pretend that this is the definitive textbook of how to start a business. This is my personal story, the story of a girl who followed her dreams. The journey that I went through was the most fulfilling and exciting that I ever imagined, and, more than a business adventure, it was a life journey. My story will show you the different steps I had to go through from starting the business to growing it to where it is right now. I want to share with you my challenges and difficulties, breakdowns and breakthroughs, victories and frustrations along the way.

There will be a lot of critics on your journey – they will question you, doubt your idea and bring you down. This was all I could hear when I started the business:

'Beauty is a competitive industry, you will never make it.'

'You don't have a beauty background.'

'Your products are nothing special, you will fail.'

'Good idea but not for us.'

'I can't understand how your products are different from any other brand.'

'You can't compete with the big brands.'

I can't pretend that I wasn't affected by these comments: they really did knock the wind out of my sails at the time. But I believed in my product, I believed I had something special and just kept going, and from time to time I'd get a positive, so that would blow away all the negatives. I'd focus on that positive comment and that gave me the energy to keep on keeping on. I was also very fortunate to have a supporting family around me who believed in me and supported me against all odds.

I made it happen and I hope to give you some inspiration so that you can do it too. There is no way I am going to sugar-coat the difficulties – as I hope you will appreciate as you follow my journey, this was not an easy ride – but I can promise you that the path I have taken is the most rewarding and fulfilling thing I have done (outside of having children and my family relationships, obviously). Even though it was hard going at times, I still believe that, should you decide to take this road yourself, it will be the most fun you've ever had.

You may think that you don't have 'The Right Stuff' to start a business. Well, I never saw myself as an entrepreneur. In fact, as you will see, starting my own business had never crossed my mind. I always thought people who started their own business were either superhuman geniuses with exceptional leadership skills, or the sort of people who started confectionery-selling empires at school and ran four different companies by the time they were 12. I certainly wasn't born an entrepreneur and never thought I quite fitted the image I had built in my mind of what an entrepreneur was, but the more so-called entrepreneurs I met, the more I realised that every single one was completely different. Driven – yes. Hard-working – for sure. Passionate – of course. But as varied in character, background and motivation as you could get. In fact, all completely normal. Entrepreneurism is not a skill that you are born with, it's a skill that you learn along the way. I knew nothing about it, I just knew that I loved my products and was passionate and dedicated to them.

The purpose of this book is to inspire you to follow your dreams. If you are just starting out in your first job, want to take your career to the next level, are thinking of changing careers, starting your own business or simply want to be the best that you can be, I hope I can show you the way through my story. At the end of every section, I get down to business with some practical advice, useful steps and lists that you can follow to help realise your dreams. I call these features 'Overnight Success Secrets', and I hope that these will kickstart your journey to becoming your own Overnight Success. Yes, I know we have already established that there really is no such thing as an 'overnight success' but it's a snappy hashtag, OK?

My journey isn't over yet and there's still a lot for me to learn ... but this is where I am right now. No book can guarantee success, but I hope you can relate to my experience and get the motivation that you need to take you to the top.

Fasten your seatbelt and enjoy the journey!

Love,
Maria

1

Getting
Started

Very few people know the journey I made towards where I am today. So where did it all start?

Since I was a little girl, back in my home town in Greece, I was interested in fashion. I'd been reading fashion magazines since I was seven years old, picking up my weekly dose from the local newsstand after school on my way to piano and French lessons. I was really passionate about clothes and always wanted to dress well. I don't think I was particularly good looking and I wore glasses (and not the cool, designer glasses I am wearing now) but I think I stood out from all the other girls in my class.

Another passion of mine was beauty. My grandmother was my biggest inspiration – she had the most perfect, flawless skin and made her own creams by mixing olive oil, beeswax and crushed pomegranate. It didn't smell or look particularly appealing but she used it every day and it seemed to work miracles!

The first beauty product I ever owned was a lip gloss. It was one of those that were in mini roll-on glass bottles and had a fake strawberry colour and fragrance. I'd apply it about every 15 seconds as I recall … I LOVED beauty and was eagerly devouring any natural beauty tips I could find in my fashion magazines – such as putting lemon juice in my hair and staying out in the sun to create natural highlights (OMG, this was ruining hair big time!), using honey and sugar for a natural scrub or making a yogurt mask for sunburned skin. Where we lived, there wasn't anywhere you could buy anything but the most basic beauty products and so necessity became the mother of invention. My girlfriends knew my passion for beauty (partly because I never stopped going on about it) and were always asking me for beauty tips, so of course I started doing a few makeovers. My specialties were Vaseline on a toothbrush to enhance lashes and mixing Nivea cream with lip gloss for a natural cheek tint ... all the tricks a teenage girl could muster!

Then, when I was about 15, it finally happened: a modern beauty store offering Clinique products opened in my home town. Oh, I was in heaven. But it wasn't just the sudden availability of real beauty products that was amazing. I loved going to that shop and looking at the women who worked there. These were modern goddesses ... made up to perfection with clean, radiant skin and beautifully made-up lips and eyes. I would love to look like them one day.

Of course, my life wasn't all beauty tips. I was still at school and working hard ... even though I wasn't really interested in academia, I was a good student and I knew I needed to study hard as my dream was to finish studying and lead an exciting life. I did well and I managed to get into the University of Athens to study English Literature. I was in the big city, and I was surrounded by all the beauty and fashion products money could buy. Unfortunately I was missing a vital element ... the money. Obviously I needed to get a job to supplement my income, but I didn't just want a pay cheque. I also wanted to do something interesting outside studying Shakespeare and Latin. It's always best to play to your strengths so I started to get the idea that I could become a fashion journalist. As I mentioned, I had already been an avid reader of fashion magazines for years, and when I mean an avid reader, I mean front to back, I was reading EVERYTHING, I knew who was who, what every column was, the name of every writer. My favourite being *Seventeen* magazine. I was also reading a lot of foreign magazines, mainly *Vogue*, *Elle* and *Glamour*, and felt that some of the edginess (namely lots of biker jackets and Doc Martens – it was a simpler time) of these trailblazing publications was missing from the Greek magazines.

I felt that *Seventeen* magazine would benefit from some more edgy shoots and content and so I sent them a letter with a bunch of ideas of what I could do for them if they took me on board. I didn't think anyone would read my letter but sent it anyway.

Within a few days I got a phone call to go and see the editor-in-chief to discuss my ideas. I couldn't believe this was happening! I dressed in all black, donned a leather jacket (always look the part of the image you want to project about yourself) and went for my meeting with the editor. I explained that I was studying but had enough time for a part-time job and would love to work for *Seventeen*. To my astonishment, they agreed! I would have to come up with the ideas and stories, get them approved and then get on with them! Within a month I had a double-page spread on the New Teenager, how they dress, where they shop and where they hang out. I was always very tuned in to trends and my articles got great reviews. What an amazing start! During my time there, I went on to do a lot of different features for them, and I loved every moment. One day I'd be styling a new shoe story and scouting locations, the next I'd be sourcing clothes and working with a photographer on a fashion shoot. I'd be interviewing celebrity hairdressers and models in the morning, then out all night covering the social pages at parties. Somewhere in between, I'd squeeze out an essay about Shakespeare, but whenever I was working for the magazine I always did more than I was asked for, worked harder than expected and went the extra step.

It was here that I started doing a bit of beauty as well, interviewing celebrities on fashion, style and their beauty routines. This, I came to realise, was the moment that I really began to get interested in the actual business of beauty. I had the thought that the products around at the time were all really quite boring and uninspiring. There were lots of brands but they all seemed to be doing the same thing... it was all about a basic cleansing soap, toner and moisturiser. It was just an observation at that point but a spark had been lit.

A trip to New York that summer was going to change my life for ever. I had never been to NY before, and as the taxi drove me into Manhattan from JFK I was in awe. The buildings, the energy, the people. Anything is possible in New York and you can be anyone you want to be. And I knew there were bigger things in life for me. I had no visa, no job, no friends in NY. But I knew it would change my future. I needed to find a way to move there.

Overnight Success Secret #1

Decide what you want

You need to ask yourself: are you where you need to be to achieve your dreams? The right city, university or job? I moved from English Literature to a job in journalism to a degree in business. My road to success wasn't a straight line: I had to try a few different things to find out what I really wanted to do with my life. I'm not advocating any job-coasting or time-wasting here – in every job I did, every step of the way I was passionate about the work and didn't do anything half-heartedly. Until I realised it wasn't for me.

It's never too late to change direction. Think about what inspires you, what motivates you, what floats your boat. Be passionate about what you do and, if you are not doing it, go for it, or if you are still not sure what your passion is, then find out. Be honest with yourself and you may come to realise that you need to make a change. It's often been said but it's worth repeating … love what you do and you'll never have to work a day in your life. You need to soul search and ask yourself the following questions:

1. Are you passionate about the industry you are in?
2. Are you excited to go to work or are you dreading it?
3. Are you willing to put in the work and the hours it takes to succeed?
4. Do you daydream of being in another job/industry?

5. Do you get inspired by people in other industries/jobs and wish you had their career path?
6. What would you do if you weren't doing your current job?
7. Are you in your current job for the right reasons?
8. If there were no consequences, would you change career right now?
9. Are you concerned with other people's reactions if you were to change careers?
10. Can you see yourself in your current career path for the next 20 years, and would this make you happy?

Answer these questions honestly . . . there's really no point in doing it any other way.

Sometimes we can get so scared of change that we try to fool ourselves, but that's a whole other self-help book. If you can ask these questions and you find that you are less than enthusiastic about your current career then it is time for a change, or at the very least a deep rethink. You only have one life but you have more than one chance to make it happy and successful so give it your best shot. It doesn't matter if you just started your first job or you are 15 years into a steady career. It took me 11 years of switching between different career paths to realise what I was good at and what I wanted to do with my life. If you are in a job or an industry that you don't love any more, it will eat at your soul, and in time even the weekends, the holidays and pay rises won't give you solace. Take the plunge, believe in yourself and follow your dreams. It is never too early and never too late. Just do it!

2

I Got Fired – So What's Next?

Steve Jobs was fired and then revolutionised the technology industry by ... coming back with the iMac, iPod, iPhone, iPad ... Michael Bloomberg was fired and then went on to create the Bloomberg empire and become the Mayor of New York. As Anna Wintour famously said, 'I think everyone should get sacked at least once. It forces you to look at yourself.' It didn't feel it at the time but it was definitely a good thing for what it taught me. It is important to have setbacks because that is the reality of life. Perfection doesn't exist.

I had finished my English degree in Athens, I had dabbled in fashion journalism, but I had decided that I needed to concentrate on getting a 'real' job ... apart from that I had decided I needed to be in New York and a degree in business got me there. It also helped that my then boyfriend and now husband, Stratis, was also studying there and he encouraged me to make the move. I convinced my parents to lend me the first year's tuition and living expenses to move to NY and study for an MBA (Masters of Business Administration) at Columbia Business School. This was one of the best times in my life. I had to study hard to keep up with a demanding course but living in New York was a dream come true. The city was full of possibilities and I loved the energy of it all. Living there made me realise that everything and anything is possible.

When I graduated two years later, I needed to find a job to pay back my study loans. The highest-paid jobs at the time for MBA graduates were from the major Wall Street investment banks. We are talking six-figure salaries and bonuses in return for your life and soul. I had no interest in banking but needed the money and my CV listed an MBA from an Ivy League school, so I was fully marketable and I decided to start applying for banking jobs.

Just what was the world of banking all about? If you watched the movie *The Wolf of Wall Street*, starring Leonardo DiCaprio, you'll have an idea of what it was like working in investment banking. I had no problem with working very hard and I was more than happy to earn huge amounts of cash, wear designer clothes and travel the world. In fact, sign me up right now, when do you want me to start? I strode out on to Wall Street, CV in hand, and I got rejected by every single bank.

On reflection, this was fair enough as I didn't actually have any relevant experience. However, I don't give in easily, a trait which has seen me in good stead through the years and one worth cultivating. I kept applying and finally got lucky. Salomon Brothers said they had a job for me. It was a surprise then but I find it miraculous now and I still don't quite understand how I managed to convince them that this is what I wanted to do with my life. Still, I was now in the world of banking and, if I'm completely honest, it was more because of the lifestyle and the aura of this exciting industry rather than any long-held dreams I had of number crunching. I wanted to hang out with Michael Douglas and Charlie Sheen … banking was a place where my life would be fast, glamorous and exciting, it was where people lived on the edge. But I had no idea what I was getting into.

I headed to London to start at Salomon Brothers' City offices. This was quite an experience: a woman in a man's world. The London office was full of men in suits and just a handful of women. It was a very competitive, sink-or-swim culture. It was all about who would stay later, who would start earlier, who could claim the least hours sleep or the longest without a day off.

It was a tough, competitive world. I had to cancel my Christmas holidays at a day's notice and was working weekend after weekend. I had zero time off and no friends.

Two years into this craziness, I wasn't loving my job or my life any more. The novelty of buying another Prada suit and flying business class all over the world had worn off. The money was great but I'd had it with the macho culture and wasn't going anywhere with my career. I mentally checked out and started taking it easy: leaving early, not showing up on weekends and (shock, horror) actually taking my holidays. Needless to say, a few months later I was fired. It wasn't a surprise but it was a shock.

This was 1999 and the first time in my life that I didn't have a job or an idea of what I would do next. My life was about to change for ever.

Overnight Success Secret #2

Get out of your comfort zone

Great things never come from comfort zones. Getting fired from a job that you don't really like is not the end of the world. Generally, there is a solid reason why someone gets fired. I have yet to see someone who is passionate about their job, who loves it, works hard and fits the company culture get fired (unless they are an alcoholic … and I have seen that too). If you get fired, you may be in the wrong industry, you may not be enjoying your work any more, you may dread going in to the office, you many not fit in the culture of the company or just not be the right fit for the role. Whatever the reason, getting fired will make you rethink what you really want to do with your life. You may realise that you want to be in a completely different industry. It may be the wake-up call that you need to make you rethink your choices; it may turn out to be the best thing that has ever happened to you.

Sometimes it's great not to have another job lined up. That time off is your opportunity to take stock, clear your head and get the inspiration to start something that could make you an overnight success. If you find yourself in this situation, it does suck at the time, but you will be better off in the long run. Sometimes we are so wrapped up in our day-to-day lives that we don't take the time to self-assess, to step outside of ourselves and ask the questions, 'Am I happy?' 'Am I on the right track?' Sometimes you need that clarity and that moment to yourself to realise 'This is not the right career path for me, I need to make a change now.'

You don't always need to get yourself fired from a job in order to change direction, but you do need a catalyst of some sort. The more complacent and comfortable you are with your current job, the longer it may take to get to a decision to take the leap. But a shock like getting fired gets you to a decision much quicker, obviously! When you do get fired, or made redundant, you are put in a 'fight or flight' situation. You need to make decisions for your future and make them quick. It can be more difficult to commit to making those decisions if it's up to you to make the leap and walk away from a job, switch industry or start your own business.

How do you know it's time for a change? Ask yourself the following questions:

1. Do you enjoy going to work every day?
2. Do you like your co-workers and boss?
3. Are you passionate about the industry you are currently in?
4. Are you proud to work for your company?
5. Does your current job fulfil you?
6. Do you ever daydream about doing another job?
7. Are you envious of people with different careers to yours?
8. Do you dislike your job but fear making a change?
9. Are you unhappy with your job but you can't get the same salary anywhere else?
10. Do you take a lot of sick days as you can't bear going to the office?

If you answer mostly NO to questions 1–5 and YES to questions 6–10, you really need to think about taking some action.

3

Beauty and Brains

I never thought I would have my own business. I don't come from a family of entrepreneurs, I had been brought up with quite the opposite philosophy ... in fact my parents always encouraged me to work for a stable, established company.

When I was in NY studying business, there was a boom in new beauty brands. Young girls were revolutionising the beauty industry and they were hotter than fashion designers. Marcia Kilgore founded Bliss, the coolest spa and beauty range in NY, Christy Turlington founded Sundari, and Jeanine Lobell founded Stila. I followed the paths and success stories of those women and dreamed of being like them. How amazing would it be to have my own beauty brand one day? I had been passionate about beauty since I was a little girl and it would be a dream come true but all I knew was the corporate world. I did not see a path to achieving it.

In an ideal world, you would have worked for one of the big beauty brands for a few years, learned the industry, made contacts and then left to set up your own beauty brand. I had just been fired from a job in banking, and apart from my stint in beauty journalism when I was at uni and the fact that I owned a fair amount of beauty products, I didn't have much more to offer. Applying for a job at a beauty brand was out of the question.

In the late nineties, the big buzz in skincare was for skin injectables and targeted treatments. Plastic surgery was becoming more common and more affordable, but now the thing that united everyone was the desire for immediate results without surgery, and injectables were the closest they could get. At the time, no one was offering any alternatives in the skincare market and I realised there was scope to do more, to make it more high tech. I knew the demand would be huge, but imagined that someone in an Estée Lauder laboratory somewhere was already well on their way to realising this goal. Maybe they were, but they hadn't done it yet. I had identified a gap in the market for a range that would offer targeted treatments for specific skin concerns. I wanted to make the range effective, luxury and fun, using bright colours and interesting packaging that would look great in your bathroom. In 1999 I set up my business with just £20,000, my husband as a co-investor and a big dream.

I spent the first year researching different labs, going to trade shows and connecting with suppliers, looking for someone who would be able to translate my ideas into products. I was very lucky to discover a London-based lab with this wonderful French chemist who immediately got my ideas and we got on very well. I worked with the lab and, within six months, I had my first formulas. Not coming from the industry, I was totally clueless about what it takes to launch a beauty brand and compete in such a saturated market. But in hindsight that worked well for me as everything I did was probably against what a traditional beauty brand would do and consequently it made Rodial stand out. I didn't have a degree in science but I knew exactly what I wanted the products to do even if I had no idea what ingredients would achieve those results.

The first step was to find a name for the range. I worked with a trademark lawyer to help me secure and trademark a name. Choosing a name for your brand is the most important thing you need to decide. It needs to be easy to pronounce, it needs to be catchy and represent the brand. At the time, pomegranate was getting a lot of buzz as the new superfood ingredient. I spoke to my lab and they researched the ingredient for me and found that it had three times the antioxidant power of green tea and vitamin C … it was one of the most powerful antioxidants known at the time. No one was using it in a big way and so we decided to use it in all our products. It was a bit of a 'Kismet' moment. I had grown up with pomegranate in my life. It was always in our house and was so evocative of my Greek childhood ... as well as being a superfood ingredient this felt like it would be good karma. The Greek word for pomegranate is *rodi* ... so I decided to call the range Rodial. It sounded French and technical and that would fit the bill.

Rodial has really evolved since its launch. With time, we started using revolutionary ingredients such as dragon's blood, bee venom and Syn-Ake peptide to combat ageing, and we became known as a key player in the skincare industry, always taking risks and revolutionising the market. Snake Serum and the Dragon's Blood Sculpting Gel became our number one best-selling products in all our retailers in the first year of launch and they are still in the top-five best-selling products in the business. Ranges such as Bee Venom, Superfood, Superacids and Pink Diamond followed, all targeting different skin types and skincare problems and all bringing something new and exciting to the skincare market.

After naming the brand Rodial, next up was deciding on the logo and packaging. I knew that for the brand to be taken seriously I needed a logo and a design for the brand and its packaging that would suit my aspirations and my vision. I did some research, took a deep breath and went to see one of the top design agencies to brief them on a design for Rodial. It cost me my entire marketing budget for that year ... a huge outlay but one I knew I needed to do. The right logo or design can last a lifetime – it sometimes can even go beyond the brand itself and become an icon on its own (Coca-Cola, Apple, Nike, the list goes on). I wasn't expecting quite that sort of impact but what I got was a huge disappointment.

The branding was miles away from what I had briefed, the text was weak and barely readable on the product. I tried to argue that it wasn't what I asked for but I had no leverage: I asked for a design, I got a design. As far as they were concerned, that was the end of that ... 'Of course, if you want us to do some more work on it we'd be happy to ... for a fee.' There was no way I could afford to do it all again. I was desperate and I was down but not out. I got out my laptop and started work. I made my own design and headed off to see my friendly neighbourhood Kall Kwik printer. I got everything printed up, it looked great and, better still, it was all free.

I had been unlucky. Not every agency will give you a design you hate. Maybe I didn't give them a good enough brief, maybe the designer had a hot date to go to and just rushed it ... I don't know, but I guess one of the lessons here is that I didn't give up and I didn't settle for something I wasn't happy with and I knew, in the long run, would not be right for my brand.

Looking back at this experience, it occurs to me that the other lesson was that I learned what the brand wasn't. I knew instantly what I didn't want when I saw it and I knew I would recognise what was right. I had started by commissioning a fancy design agency but who could possibly know this brand better than me? If I were to go to that agency now, I am pretty sure they'd nail it because I would know exactly what to say about the look, feel and personality of my brand. Back then, maybe I wasn't so capable of articulating those things, but I knew them in my heart and you will know the same things about your brand too.

The other key question when you start your own business is obviously where you will be based. There is no point in investing in fancy offices when you start. First of all, there is no excess cash available to invest in luxuries and you want every pound that you spend to go on something that will have a return on your investment. I needed to invest in product and PR and save on rent. I based the company from a 3 x 1m back room at home, which could fit a narrow desk with shelves and two cupboards. It was great that I even had this room and could allocate it. This was the Rodial headquarters for the first few years.

I couldn't pay rent or even a salary for myself and I asked my husband, Stratis, to support me while I was getting the business off the ground. He couldn't have been more supportive and we decided we would co-own the business. He was a silent partner at the beginning, fully supporting the cash-flow needs rather than us having to rely on an external investor, but when the business took off in 2012 he came on board full time and became the Chief Finance Officer.

I often get asked why I didn't take external investment, as the company is still privately owned by the two of us. We have had people knocking on our door from the early stages up to now – we get approached by private equity funds as well as some big-name brands interested in the business. Perhaps if we took funding earlier, we would have had a lot more cash to fund exciting things and perhaps even grow faster. We didn't get external investment for two reasons. One is that I am really passionate about what I do and I didn't start the business with an exit plan in mind. When I meet people and tell them about the business, they sometimes ask, 'So what is your end goal?' I didn't know how to answer this the first few times … I am expected to say that the end goal is to grow the business as much as I can and sell it to a big beauty conglomerate, and then retire and be on constant holidays. I don't really have a goal, and, like everything in life, it's all about the journey rather than the destination, right? If anything, my goal is to go to work every day, be creative, inspire my team and come up with revolutionary beauty products that help women feel beautiful and confident. If along the way we make a profit and I am able to enjoy some nice things for myself and an occasional holiday, so be it. But I didn't get into this for the money. Being an entrepreneur is not a get-rich-quick scheme – that was never on my agenda.

The second reason we didn't get investment was that I know exactly what I need to do to drive the business. I have the instinct on many things and can juggle a lot of balls to make things happen. I have heard horror stories over the years of private equity companies investing in a business, having a say in a lot of decisions and then ruining the companies. Let's not forget that the aim of private equity firms is to grow the business to the next level and then sell to someone else. This is how they make their money. So, unless the entrepreneur is of the same mindset there will be a struggle, with the entrepreneur almost always losing and being left out of the business that they started with their own blood, sweat and tears. The only way that external investment works is if both the entrepreneur and the private equity firm are on a mission to cash out – then everyone is on the same page and happy.

Another benefit of not getting an external investor is that you are more careful with how you spend your money. Since day one at Rodial, we would spend what we had and with some help from Stratis and a bank overdraft we managed to fund our growth very conservatively. You become very resourceful and very good at assessing return on investment, which makes the company profitable sooner. Once we started making a bit more and turning a profit, a big part of it still went back into the business to fund growth, and it still does. I see companies who have received tons of outside investment and gone on crazy growth spurts but have no profits yet, and this is a very dangerous position to be in.

When I set up the business, my first hire was a part-time accountant (who is still at the business and is now our Group Financial Controller and longest-standing member of the team!) so I could focus on product, PR and sales and not have to deal with accounting. It was a really neat operation but that meant that I had low overheads and could expand or scale down as the business went through different stages during the first few years. It was pretty tight but it worked. Since then, we have moved three times to bigger offices but only when it became absolutely necessary. We now have some beautiful offices with lots of glass and light and minimal desks, a breakout room where the teams gather together to get inspiration and a studio for shoots and filming. We've come a long way!

In the start-up phase, it took me a year from the moment I decided to set up my business to receiving boxes of products in my tiny office. How exciting! I was ready for business! All it would take was to write a few emails, make a few calls and my products would land on the shelves of Harrods, Harvey Nichols and Space NK. Well, not quite.

This goes back to my lack of experience in the beauty industry. I didn't realise how hard it would be to get my products into the stores. The stores don't just look at a pretty product and packaging with an interesting story. They need to see the press behind the product, how you can support it with salespeople and events, and they need to make space by removing another underperforming brand. And once you are there, you need to deliver the sales that the stores require in order to stay on the shelves. If I was coming from the beauty industry and realised how much work it takes, I would probably not have done it. But again, my naivety helped me a long way.

I started contacting the stores to carry my range. This is the hardest thing. I was emailing and calling everyone –

Harvey Nichols, Harrods, Selfridges, Space NK. Naturally no one was taking my calls. I begged and hustled and called and emailed again, and finally a miracle happened. We launched Rodial on a tiny shelf in Fenwick on Bond Street, London. When I saw the products on the shelf for the first time, I couldn't believe it! These were MY products on the shelves of a major department store! This was really happening ... I was an entrepreneur!

Overnight Success Secret #3

Is Entrepreneurship the Right Career for You?

So you have come to the point of realising you are in a dead-end job or career, and decide you want to venture out on your own. You could be setting up a new business for a new product or service, or want to grow the brand that is you. All of these qualify you as an entrepreneur. How do you know if this is the right risk for you or total craziness? Are entrepreneurs born or made?

The good news is that there aren't any universal traits that make someone more likely to succeed as an entrepreneur. Entrepreneurs come in different shapes and forms. Peter Drucker, the entrepreneurship expert and author, says, 'It is not a personality trait: In thirty years, I have seen people of most diverse personalities and temperaments perform well in entrepreneurial challenges. Some entrepreneurs are egocentric and others are painfully correct conformist. Some are fat and some are lean. Some are worriers and some are relaxed . . . some have great charm and some have no more personality than a frozen mackerel!'

Since there is no specific entrepreneurial personality, anyone can become one and master the skills needed to succeed. Once you start making decisions and plans and you are in charge of your own destiny, you can learn to be an entrepreneur. If you have an idea, you pursue it and you have the drive to do whatever it takes to turn your dream into reality. This is the starting point and you learn to be an entrepreneur along the way. The only tools you need are persistence, hard work and determination. And your drive will be your passion to make your idea a reality.

I didn't have any experience when I started my business. I learned everything along the way. At times I would learn from mistakes and other times I got it right straight away. I wasn't trained or experienced in beauty manufacturing or marketing beauty products. I had never sold a product in my life. By starting the business, you learn as you go along and you become better and smarter with every decision you make, whether right or wrong.

The lack of industry experience can be your biggest advantage. Being clueless allows you to focus on the end products and be totally unaware of the challenges that you would face along the way. It makes you think out of the box, whether through new ideas or ways to get things done on a tight budget. The key thing is to understand your strengths and weaknesses and learn fast. Try to teach yourself the skills that you are missing or get a consultant on board or, if you can afford it, hire people with complementary skills to yours.

Anyone can be an entrepreneur, but this is not a career for everyone. Being an entrepreneur is not just a career, it's a lifestyle choice. It's a very emotional and very time-consuming commitment, and you have to be ready for it. You are doing what you love … you control your future, but you are also bringing a huge amount of uncertainty into your life and you can never switch off. Your business and your life are one.

One of the reasons not to become an entrepreneur is if your main goal is to get rich quick. Yes, a lot of entrepreneurs end up rich but if this is your only drive you will be massively disappointed. You need to be passionate about your idea, enjoy the hard work, and the money may or may not come. If money is your single motivation, then your business will most likely fail.

Some questions to ask yourself to see if entrepreneurship is right for you:

1. Are you ready for a 24-hours-a-day job?
2. Would you still start the business if you had to sacrifice your big salary for a few years and put all the money back into the business?
3. Are you happy to be responsible for your employees and deal with all their issues?
4. Are you ready to go out there and sell your dream?
5. Can you deal with multiple rejections and still keep going?
6. Are you ready to roll up your sleeves and get everything done, including menial tasks?
7. Can you cope with uncertainty?
8. Are you willing to work extremely hard for a very long time?
9. Can you keep going after a lot of rejections and disappointment?
10. Are you ready to get out of your comfort zone?

Anyone can be an entrepreneur if they really want. The question is, are you ready for it? If you are, nothing is going to stop you!

4

Daily Struggle

During the first few years of the business I was doing everything, literally everything, myself. I worked out of the tiny spare bedroom and bought some IKEA cupboards to store the stock. I would go to the Starbucks around the corner every morning for a soy-milk cappuccino and would sit with my laptop writing down ideas on how to get my business off the ground. In fact, looking back on it now, Starbucks did play a huge role in my business, I just didn't realise it at the time. As well as giving me a daily shot of caffeine-fuelled energy, the Starbucks of central London doubled as my temporary office, boardroom and meeting room. I had an encyclopaedic knowledge of which ones were near my regular clients and when certain branches were quieter than others (FYI in the City they are crazy in the early morning but business dies down from around 10am, but in Covent Garden they are quieter early and get busy as the tourists arrive) ... I held interviews there, I did research and I drank a lot of coffee. But these were early days and I wasn't holding a lot of meetings in Starbucks or anywhere else, in fact. I was sending more emails and making more calls than I was receiving, dealing with suppliers on orders and packaging, having meetings with the lab to discuss new products, invoicing and doing some basic accounting.

I even worked in the 'warehouse'. That is to say, I packed and mailed everything myself at home. Once I started to get some sales I had to get the product delivered ... and Starbucks, good as they were, did not supply a post and packing service, even to their most loyal customers. So, among the Christmas wrapping parcels, twinkling lights and star-topped tree, our Christmas décor also featured stacks of product and boxes. There was no other way this was going to happen: I was packing, labelling and cataloguing all the last-minute deliveries myself at home, and this wasn't a one-off. As the business grew, this became a regular Christmas ritual for a few years, including the odd 24-hour packaging session, but it's surprising how time flies when you are passionate about what you do.

Another skill I had to develop over the first few years was going to the stores and selling my products. I must confess that I have a slight problem with selling to customers. I have no problem sitting down at a corporate meeting and pitching for a few hundred thousand pounds of orders. But I have a big problem trying to sell an individual consumer a pot of one of my creams. I would rather give it for free. Despite my fear, I had to deliver sales for the stores and made myself sell!

This was one of the scariest things I have ever done. I really had to beg and plead for sales as I was an unknown brand and had to deal with rejection and days of not selling a single product. On the plus side, this really pushed me out of my comfort zone and brought me closer to my customer, and allowed me to get first-hand feedback. I still get an energy buzz from going to the stores now – my teams are doing all the hard work for me, but I still love to engage with the end consumer. Even now, when my key store teams email me at the end of their day, it is one of my favourite emails.

You would think that launching in one store was all you needed and the rest of the retailers would take on the products and follow suit. Well, not quite. I would hassle the buyers of my favourite stores (Harvey Nichols, Space NK, Harrods and Selfridges) once every quarter. If I ever got an email from them saying 'stop emailing me', I would stop but, until then, I wouldn't take no for an answer.

Harrods was the first store we got on board. I met with the glamorous head of fashion and beauty, Marigay

McKee, over lunch a few times and she agreed to stock Rodial products. I was ecstatic. Harvey Nichols wasn't as easy. It took me a couple more years until I finally got Daniela Rinaldi, Concessions and Beauty Director at Harvey Nichols, to agree to take the products on board in their apothecary department. Another huge milestone for the brand.

The hardest one to get was Space NK. This is a chain of upscale beauty boutiques offering cool and niche beauty brands, and had around 50 locations at the time. I invited their founder Nicky Kinnaird for breakfast at Ceconni's in Mayfair to introduce her to Rodial. She accepted (I couldn't believe it!) and you would think she would be ready to place that order. Well, it wasn't that simple. I had to finance another few breakfasts over the years and finally she agreed to take Rodial. Now we are all set, right? Not quite. The catch was that Space NK were only interested in four of our products and they would test the market in a few stores. If they did well, they would roll out the others. The problem was that the products they wanted were for bodycare and we all know these are seasonal products that perform really well during the summer, but what do you do in the winter? I decided to work hard to make those sales so that we could establish a relationship and then work from there to introduce our core products. I did whatever I had to do to make this work: I was in the stores every day and hired a couple of other people to help, I gave them tons of PR credits, and I was practically sleeping at Space NK to make it work! And it paid off in the end.

It took a total of seven years for Rodial to be launched in Harvey Nichols, Harrods, Selfridges and Space NK in the UK. Dring that time, we also expanded internationally to the US, Europe and Asia. Now Rodial is available in over 2,000 luxury stores, including Saks Fifth Avenue, in 35 countries worldwide. Hard work was paying off. Working hard means sacrificing other areas of your life; it's simply a question of how much you are willing to sacrifice for success. There are no shortcuts.

I often get asked how did you go from setting up a business in a back room at home to building a beauty empire? A lot of hard work but also a number of risks that paid off. A few years into the business, in 2005, I got a call from an agency in LA that was organising goodie bags for a major after-party at the Oscars. They had heard of a product that we just launched called Tummy Tuck (a body product to tighten the skin around the tummy area), and they thought it sounded really cool and wanted to include it in the goodie bag. This was a time when it was really hard to get products in a goodie bag and it was a big deal to be asked. They needed 2,000 pieces, which was a huge number for us at the time as our usual production run was just 1,000 for the whole year! But I thought this would be a great opportunity to get the product and our brand into the hands of the influencers (actors were THE influencers at the time; there were no beauty bloggers or TV personalities in 2005 or, if there were, they were not that influential in those pre-social media times). I took the risk and ordered a lot more. And the risk paid off. The party was attended by tons of celebrities including Jennifer Aniston, Tom Cruise and Katie Holmes, so Rodial got a lot of attention and publicity.

Another pivotal point into my journey, which again involved taking a risk, was when I launched our first ever anti-ageing serum. I like to read up about all the ingredients and research that have gone into test samples, and I came across a great, key ingredient called Syn-Ake peptide. Reading further, I found out that this peptide mimics the reaction to a snake bite resulting in a mild freeze-like effect in facial muscles. I became really excited about this story and thought, why not shout about this and actually name the product Snake Serum? And not only did we name the product Snake Serum but we took it to the next level. We did a photoshoot with real snakes, which created much excitement. We had no budget to advertise but there was a lot of buzz about this product and people started talking about Rodial.

The Dragon's Blood range (dragon's blood is sap from a tree rather than something from a scene in *Game of Thrones* …) followed, which created even more excitement for the brand and is still one of our top-selling ranges.

A third pivotal moment for Rodial was the launch of a new makeup range in 2014. Rodial started as a skincare range and, over 16 years, we have grown our skincare business to over 30 products, tackling every possible skincare concern from fine lines and wrinkles to dehydration, sun spots, dark circles, neck, lips and lashes. How could I take the business to the next level? I saw a gap in the makeup market and I had to go after it …

Having been in the skincare business for 16 years, you would think that it would be an easy task. Call your factories and tell them what you want and you'll have a new makeup range in no time. Well, it's a lot more complicated than that. The contract manufacturers that do skincare are very different to the ones that do makeup. And while the UK has a good selection of skincare fillers and labs, there aren't any good makeup manufacturers. So there I was, almost like starting from scratch, visiting trade shows and understanding the colour market.

A lot of makeup ranges are created by makeup artists and are mostly suitable for use by other makeup artists, so they can be intimidating for the rest of us.

Too many colours, textures, options. Every time I would sit for a makeover at MAC or Bobbi Brown, I would love the look and buy tons of staff but then I would go home and wouldn't know how to replicate it. My idea was to come up with formulas and textures that were sheer and light even for the most heavy-handed customers, and to educate every single customer on how to replicate the look at home. I wanted a range that was easy to use and apply, and I wanted to be able to show every one of our customers how to achieve a flawless look with just a few products in just a few minutes. I was looking at the makeup of the hottest celebrities and models and loved the idea of sculpting and contouring as a trend and incorporated that into our range.

I was really excited about the idea of a new Rodial makeup range. I felt like I was launching a new brand all over again. It took me three years from coming up with the idea to launching the range. I spent a lot of time trying to source the best formulas in France, Italy and Switzerland as well as developing our unique packaging. A lot of skincare brands that launch makeup fail as they treat it as an extension of skincare. My vision was to create a makeup brand that could sit by itself, have its own identity and not depend on the existence of skincare.

I spent a lot of time designing our packaging and created bespoke compacts with textures and beautiful shiny hardware. I worked with the best factories in Europe to create a stunning collection that would stand on its own.

After three years in development, the Rodial sculpting makeup range was ready in the early summer 2014. I emailed one of our big supporters over the years, Daniela Rinaldi at Harvey Nichols, and we met within a week so that I could present the new range. Very direct as always, Daniela said to me: 'How can we pitch for this?' Excuse me? I thought to myself, what do you mean? I couldn't believe it. It turned out that Daniela not only got the concept, but she also liked it so much that she wanted it exclusively in her store. I said, give us a week and our marketing team will put together a marketing plan so we can get the exclusive counter and sculpting bar in Harvey Nichols Knightsbridge. I couldn't have been happier.

We were given two months to design and fit the counter, which was to be in the middle of the store next to YSL, Estée Lauder and Tom Ford. OMG, we were playing with the big boys! We would be taking over the space from a US spa line that looked really sad and always empty. Within a couple of months and with no previous experience in setting up counters, we installed our first flagship counter and sculpting bar. I didn't have anyone in the business with experience in designing and project managing counters (and it wouldn't make sense to hire a specialist just for this one). So, as usual, I project managed this on my own, treating the design as if it was part of my own home.

During the time of the design, I happened to be in NY and went into Barneys and Saks and took lots of pictures of the counters I liked and was emailing the designer constantly. I ended up holding the designer's hand and choosing all the elements of the scheme myself. We used a dark grey colour to make the counter less harsh than black, and the light fittings are similar to the Tom Dixon ones I have at home. I wanted to give the counter a warm and homely feel with stools that have the same grey chenille material and beige piping as my sofa at home.

When we launched the counter, everyone at Harvey Nichols was very impressed and they couldn't believe how we had transformed and maximised the space. I have a soft spot for this counter and I love to visit and chat with my team, finding out about customer feedback and listening to suggestions while having my makeup done by our professional makeup artists. We use the space to host customer, press and blogger events and it is truly our home. Needless to say, I am very proud of it.

A year later, our counter sales mean that we are regularly within the top ten best-selling brands in Harvey Nichols London, and at times we are ahead of Chanel, YSL and Tom Ford. It is a great feeling to have your idea trusted by a retailer and then to prove to them that you can make it happen. The launch went so well that we rolled out to all the Harvey Nichols regional stores within a year.

With every new project I took on with Rodial, I had to think out of the box and make up the lack of funds with creativity and by taking constant risks. Success is about the relentless pursuit of what you want and hard work is an essential ingredient. Those who are just after a get-rich-quick scheme and are not willing to put in the hard work are likely to fail.

You will need to work non-stop. Monday to Friday, nine to six, is just about dealing with the day-to-day operation of your business. All your creative work will need to be done before nine and after six and during weekends. There won't be time for hobbies, and forget about extended holidays. You may not have time for a social life or to cultivate friendships outside work (and even if you do, the non-stop, 'no sleep-till-Brooklyn' side of your personality will be wondering, 'What can this person do to help my business?'). It's a choice that you will have to make and you need to be comfortable with these sacrifices.

I may be exhausted after flying the red eye from NY and landing at Heathrow at 7am, but I go straight to the office as I need to connect with my team and check up on how they have been doing. Am I exhausted? Yes. Do

I have a coffee and just get on with my day? Absolutely! I could make a case to myself that 'Hey, it's my business, I'm the boss, I'll take the rest of the day off ...' and as I AM the boss no one is going to argue. But if you want success, there is no time for that. I have been known to fly to Japan for 24 hours for a meeting, and then as soon as the meeting is over I'm back in a cab to the airport and flying back to London. Why not stay in Japan for day, or even a week? Adjust to the time difference, take a day shopping, absorb some culture? I'll tell you why. Travelling is not a hobby. I need to be back to catch up with my team, attend meetings and be back with my family. Family is important. I'm not a COMPLETE machine!

Quite simply, if you really want to succeed, you never really switch off. It's not that you can't switch off, it's that you don't want to! If this is your passion, if this is what you want, you'll find yourself switched on all the time ... it will be a natural extension of your love for your business. It won't even be a conscious decision.

When I am not in the office, whether I am at home or travelling or even if I find myself miraculously enjoying a free weekend, and an email comes in that for whatever reason needs a quick response, of course I will respond back, any day, any time. Same goes for important calls. Obviously, I restrict these to legitimate 'can't wait' issues, but the fact remains that I am never really turned off from my business.

Now, you may have read a lot of articles about this kind of behaviour in the press – people checking emails by the pool and heading for an early stress-related grave, etc. Well, yes, I am sure that is a valid point but I refer you to my earlier comment that this not a job, it's a passion. I am not trying to impress the boss or win a promotion, or worried that I'll be replaced by that young go-getter in accounts.

This is my business, so to me it's no pressure at all. I'm available because I want to be. Because I care about my business. We are operating across several different time zones, from the US to Asia to Australia, so things do tend to happen 24/7 and a quick response often saves a lot of time in the long run. It doesn't mean that I am up all night responding to emails: some things can wait and some things I am happy to leave to my team. After all, what's the point of having them if you can't delegate? But I am generally available when I have to be. I am yet to find a massively successful person who works nine-to-five and switches off after work.

Sometimes I may hit a wall and find myself worn down and mentally exhausted. Despite my tough talk, I am only human and something has to give. All I need is a good night's sleep, a good workout in the morning and I am back to action with even more energy. You need to find your own release valve and know when to let off the pressure. This isn't a sign of weakness (I am thinking back to the macho 'who's done the most all-nighters?' culture of my banking days here), it should be part of your plan. Recognise (or take the word of someone you trust, usually your partner or PA) when you are flagging and need to step back, refresh and regroup. You need the energy and the self-discipline to go all night for sure, but also to manage your time and get the balance right.

Having said that, your resistance to tiredness may be greater simply because, if you love it, it won't seem like work. So you'll find you can go on longer than you would in a job you despise, or even are a just a bit 'meh' about.

If you ask me to do a crossword puzzle, I might fill in a few squares, doodle in the margin for a bit, and get a bit excited that I know the answer to 6 down ... but ultimately I will just get bored and give up. I hate crosswords. So it is in all things: you need to really love it, want it and enjoy it … this is what will give you the self-discipline to achieve it. If you pursue something that you are passionate about, that passion will keep you going. Pick a career that you love so much that you won't even consider doing something else.

Working hard isn't just about the amount of time and the sacrifices that you need to make. It is also about which areas outside your area of expertise are you willing to explore. As an entrepreneur, you pretty much need to have a rounded understanding of everything: from your product to sales and marketing, from operations to finance and legal. Yes, you can hire experts and consultants, but you should be able to move out of your comfort zone and your traditional expertise and at least get a basic grasp on these areas. You need to know what they are talking about in the meetings and you want to be able to quiz them to make sure they are doing the very best for your business … don't be in the dark about anything. Remember, you are the captain of this ship and you need to be familiar with every rivet.

When you start a business you have no choice but to be hands on. You are most likely cash-strapped and you need to stretch yourself pretty thin to fill all of those holes. You are the sales manager, the operations manager, the accountant and the admin assistant all rolled into one. You may even answer the phone in a different voice and pretend to be your own PA … I certainly did! As you grow and the business becomes more stable, you hire your first employees, usually people who have complementary skills to yours so, between all of you, you cover all bases. And there comes a time when your business has a lot more people and you have your managers and you have taken a step back. So now you can sit back and relax and let everyone else do the job for you? You worked hard all those years, surely it's time to let others do their share of the hard work? Not quite.

As much as you trust the people around you, you need to be on top of things and occasionally dig a bit deeper in every department to find out what is going on. There are times that your people won't share something with you because a) they want to show that they are on top of things, b) they don't think it's important, or c) they think you don't care.

From this digging and the accumulation of small bits of seemingly unimportant information you sometimes strike gold. You may get an idea for a new product, find the solution to a problem or understand where the roadblocks to the business lie.

So how do you find this stuff out? How can you keep on top of all the little things when you are so consumed with your own job, taking the company places, driving the big vision, global domination, etc? The way I do it (and I know a lot of businesses do the same) is by holding 'The Monday Morning Meeting'. This is a regular, permanent fixture in everybody's calendar where I get the heads of all departments to go through their past week and talk about their plans for the upcoming week. This is a meeting where I get them to do the talking. Everyone has a chance to have their say and offer solutions to any issues and it gives everyone an understanding of 'where we are now' and a platform from which to follow up. It's also an excellent way to get everyone connected with the other departments. Some people naturally communicate more, either because they are closely connected in the business model or their sections are next to each other in the office . . . or simply because they are friends. Obviously, though, there are those who, without this meeting, might never make meaningful contact. The business might be just fine if they carried on in their own worlds, but having the right hand know what the left hand is doing is, as you might expect, very beneficial.

It's not just about keeping tabs on what's going on: knowing what everyone else is up to gives the business a great sense of cohesion. We are all singing from the same hymn sheet and are in tune. The airing of all of this information has another benefit: it gives your staff a sense of ownership, they feel part of the bigger vision. If they can see the whole picture instead of being limited to their little corner, they have an opportunity to be more creative, more visionary and more engaged themselves.

In addition to the formal Monday meetings, if it's quiet I might take people out for coffee or lunch and check up on them in a more informal setting, or just call them into my office for a five-minute catch-up. I try to connect with all departments as often as I can and, when I have a trip, I try to organise things so I can still be in the office for the Monday morning meeting. If a week goes by without that meeting I feel disconnected from the team.

There will be times that you will have worked really hard, made the sacrifices, but still you are not getting the results that you want. Do you give up?

With every challenge, every disappointment, think to yourself: Why am I doing this? What is the big picture? What would success look like if I keep going? Have the big picture always in mind.

I have to admit there are times that I am overwhelmed. A product launch isn't as successful as anticipated, certain team members are driving me crazy with how high maintenance they are, some buyers are irrational with their requests and sometimes this all happens within a day.

What keeps me going? I take a step back and think about the big picture. Think about how I love the industry I am in, think about what success looks like, and also think of where I started. Sometimes I spend so much time on a project that, when I finally step back, I have a tendency to think I've got nothing to show for all the hard work and effort. That's when I have to remind myself to look back at where I started with the project and I am always pleasantly surprised with the progress. It's about perspective.

Overnight Success Secret #4

Face Your Fears

Let's be honest. Fear is horrific and paralysing. Fear when you are an entrepreneur is commonplace. Fear of failure, fear of success and fear of the unknown. Will I have enough cash to pay my staff? Will I grow fast? Will I be better than my competition? Will the deals fall through? Will the clients be unhappy? Will the suppliers fall through? Will someone sue us?

Fear can come at you at any time. It's how the brain processes fear that can take it out of proportion.

Fear holds so many people back in life. Fear of the unknown, fear of not being good enough, fear of failing – I went through them all. It is so much easier to avoid fear and keep on doing what makes you feel comfortable. Fear comes from a negative experience that you may have had in the past and you think that if you experience the same situation again you will get the same negative feeling. It becomes a barrier to realising your goals.

In order to face your fears, you need to remove those barriers and push past the fear. It is crucial to surround yourself with people who believe in your abilities and help you in your journey of facing your fears. You can't face your fears in one go. It is a process. It's overcoming little by little and feeling slightly more confident every time. And when you look back at when you started, you will realise the huge progress that you made.

These are my top ten tips for facing your fears.

1. Identify your fear.
2. Imagine the worst-case scenario if your fear comes true.
3. Write down all the implications.
4. Read the implications one by one and think, 'Would it be the end of the world if x happened?'
5. Put a date in your diary of the day that you will take the first step to face your fear.
6. Make sure it's a day and a time when you can focus 100 per cent on this task and there are no other pressing issues to take care of.
7. Mondays and early in the day are good options when our power of goodwill is the strongest.
8. Tell a good friend or a family member about it and ask them to be there to support you.
9. Go through further steps to address this fear.
10. Congratulate yourself with every step you take and record your progress.

5

Hiring
Smarter
People
than Me

I have never been happier with my team at Rodial. I have a team of hardworking, passionate and talented people working for me. Some of them have been with the business for more than ten years. Any time there is a job ad we get hundreds of applications to fill the position. There is so much talent out there and I can now pick the best of the best. It wasn't always like that, though.

Since I started the business I have hired and fired many times. Over the years, I have seen it all!

Rodial is not a traditional nine-to-five company. Everyone here works really hard and, while we do not encourage anyone to stay in the office late, there are from time to time a few people who might stay late, wrapping up presentations, finishing designs or doing research. And there are a lot of others who arrive well before nine to start going through their work with a clear head before everyone else arrives. Everyone is ready to roll up their sleeves and get any kind of work done if it's needed. When a company grows at the rate that we have, there are always a few holes and I expect all my team to get these covered.

I remember a time a few years ago when we suddenly got a huge wave of press on Snake Serum. It was great but it was also unexpected ... and as a consequence it was insane. We suddenly had hundreds of thousands of people going on our site to check out this miraculous product and buy it. We'd never had this amount of traffic in the past and our website at the time wasn't designed to cope with it. We had gone from a handful of visits a day to hundreds of thousands. The site crashed. We didn't have a customer services person in the team, let alone a customer services department. With the website down, the phones were ringing non-stop from customers wanting to purchase the serum but couldn't get it online. We were losing sales here ... this looked like our big leap forwards and we were losing it.

While the phones rang off the hook, I sat the whole office down and gave them a basic training in how to take an order on the phone, and suddenly I had the biggest customer services team. Everyone, and I mean everyone, had to be ready and available to take orders regardless of whether they were the managing director, the PR assistant or the office cat. Everyone was going to have to help out to get us through until we had the site up and running again. It was one of the best days we had as a team that year ... everyone was happy to help, everyone was buzzing on the 'action-stations' atmosphere and the whole office was excited to be part of this challenge. I knew then I had a great team. When I hear people saying 'This is not my job' – that is a red flag for me. Is this person right for the business?

It's not all sunshine and lollipops, though. As an entrepreneur, you sometimes need to make a tough decision. There is one I shall never forget. We had been growing for a couple of years and even though we were still small we were holding our own and I was building a loyal team around me. But these are the times when businesses can be at their most vulnerable. I had gone from doing near enough everything myself to paying staff wages and office rent and upfront production costs ... it was a big leap, and looking at the figures one night I realised we had stretched too far. No matter how I juggled it, the cash flow just would not work. Money was tight ... and I had to let some staff go. These were people who'd stayed late, who'd worked hard to keep us going, but if the business was to survive I had to bite the bullet and tell them to go. It was bad enough having to tell two of my team there was no longer a job for them. What made it worse was that this was only a couple of weeks before Christmas. Yes … I was the Grinch. I absolutely hated myself but things had got so tight with cash I am sure that the business would not have survived.

As a start-up you will not attract the resources that you need for many reasons. A lot of great employees may be put off because they need to be in a stable company and a start-up presents uncertainty in terms of both job security and job description. When you start a new business, you need people who are street smart, who have the same vision as you. Since you will be tight with cash, you need them to think out of the box and come up with ideas to get things done that don't cost a lot.

When you start, you will also need people who are flexible. In a small business the roles are not very well defined. When I started I had an accountant who as well as doing the books was also in charge of production, legal and office management. And an office assistant who would also assist on PR, social media and the web. Why would these people want to work for you when there are so many stable jobs out there? Because they believe in our brand and you give them the opportunity to work in a start-up, get the energy and the satisfaction of seeing a baby brand grow. They take part in the excitement without taking a massive risk, although they may not have the long-term job security an established company might offer. It also gives them the opportunity to learn different parts of the business, expand their skill-set and also work closely with you, the founder. They buy into your passion and drive and this can be very addictive.

How do you go about hiring people when you first start? I didn't have a budget to hire a recruitment agency (and still to this day I would much rather get a candidate through other avenues rather than having to pay a hefty 15 per cent fee on someone's yearly salary). When I started we didn't have social media and our main recruiting platform was Gumtree. We would advertise for a job for £25 and get hundreds of CVs, which is great, but then how do you choose? A lot of applications will be an immediate no based on what they say on the covering letter. I would then narrow it down to the top five and invite them for an interview. Historically 20 per cent don't show up (as Woody Allen said, turning up is 90 per cent of getting the job). When you are down to the top three, it's about how you connect with them at the interview.

It's all about personal relationships and how they would fit with the team. I made a lot of mistakes hiring the wrong people over the years. Once the skills are there (and you hope no one lies on the CV), there are a few questions that I always ask. More often than not, you are faced with candidates who, on paper at least, all seem ideally suited . . . so you end up looking for reasons NOT to hire someone rather than to hire. If, at the end of the interview, there are no reasons not to hire, then you are on to something. I try to see people at least twice. Sometimes the candidate would put on a great show at the first interview and are more relaxed on the second when they think they almost have the job and you get to really see where they are. What I like to do now is to get a few more people from my team to attend the interview, even if they wouldn't necessarily work with this person. We have a very strong culture and I like to see what my team's perception is of this new candidate.

My motto is: Hire slow and fire fast. Take your time to hire. It's an important decision. I used to hire people in a rush because there was a job opening, and then regretted it as it was the wrong choice. I now never rush a hiring decision even if that means that a position may remain open for a few months until we get the right candidate.

Overnight Success Secret #5

Interviewing Tips

Your team can make or break your business. I spend most of my time recruiting, coaching and motivating my team as it's the most important element of the company. First things first, take time to find the right candidates and don't rush any decisions. Over the years I have interviewed hundreds of people for all areas of the business and I have come up with some no-nos that help me quickly identify the best.

My checklist for red flags when interviewing a candidate:

1. Has the candidate had long stretches of time being with one company? You don't want the ones who jump from one job to another every few months as they may do the same with you.
2. Are there any large unexplained gaps in someone's CV? There are, of course, cases when a candidate needs to take some time off from the work they don't enjoy in order to make plans for their next career move and, as you know, I am all for that. However, there are people who are just not meant to work at a full-time committed job and crack under pressure. A large number of unexplained gaps may indicate to me a lack of work ethic, and when things get tough they give up.
3. Is the covering letter specific to your company and the position? You want to choose someone really

interested in the brand and the job, rather than suspecting that this is the same application they have fired off for 100 positions.

4. What is the tone of the covering letter? A number of candidates say, 'I'd like to get this job to get experience to help me with my future career.' You want to hear what THEY will bring to the table rather than what they want to get from you.

5. How far from the office do they live? We lost some great people, having spent a lot of time training them and integrating them into the team, only to lose them shortly afterwards as the commute was too long.

6. How do they talk about previous jobs? I have sat through several interviews where the candidate has badmouthed their previous employers in excruciating detail. If they do this for the previous employer, you could be next.

7. Do their answers to your questions seem like they came from a textbook? You want to see who they really are and they may be trying to hide something.

8. Ask them what other jobs they are applying for. I prefer to hear that it's not that many, and that your position is their priority, would be their dream come true, etc, rather than you are just one of ten possibilities and they'll take whatever they are offered. It's slightly different if they are all jobs in your specific industry ... at least you know they are passionate about the topic, but still you'd like them to be excited by your brand.

9. Avoid candidates with too many complicated personal problems. Not that you would ask them

during the interview, but there are candidates who explain in detail their complicated personal situation. It shows me that they have a lot going on with their lives and makes me question whether they would be focused on work.

10. Ask yourself, if I was on a plane with this person for seven hours, would I enjoy spending time with them? As this may happen, you need to make sure you get along.

6

Risks that
Paid off

The road to success is not a straight line. You need to take some risks and you need to take some tough decisions. You can manage your risks by starting with something small, and once you get more confidence take the next risk and so on, building your risk tolerance and going bigger and better each time. It doesn't always mean taking all your savings and investing them in that crazy idea (sometimes it does ...) but it could be taking the risk to change industries, start a new job or leave your job and start a small business from your spare room like I did.

What you can see from my story is that all I did was take risks that led me to where I am today. I took a risk to leave my home town and move to a big city to study. While studying, I took the risk to put myself out there and got a job in a magazine. When I realised I needed more business education, I took a risk to move to NY and study business. I then took a risk to work in a completely new industry, finance, and move to London. And after three years in that job, I took the risk of losing my high salary to start my own business. Do all risks pay off? Of course not. But all the risks you take build up your confidence, making it easier to take further risks.

By 2010, Rodial had been running for ten years. It became a household name in the luxury market. Over the years, we were getting a lot of requests from some of the more mass retailers who wanted to create an upscale apothecary feel within their beauty aisles. They had already taken some of the upscale brands on board such as Philosophy and Bare Escentuals to create these niche areas within the stores, and now they were all asking for Rodial too as it was such an innovative brand offering treatments targeted to specific skin concerns. No one else was offering anything remotely similar to it.

At that time, the high-street/luxury brand collaboration was becoming very in vogue. Stella McCartney designed a range for Gap, Lanvin and Karl Lagerfeld collaborated with H&M and Missoni collaborated with Target. It was all about creating a range that would share the DNA with the luxury brand in a more basic format. This way the customer would get exposed to the luxury brand with the hope that they would later upgrade to it. And not to mention great PR as well as a new source of revenue for the luxury brand.

Since I had a lot of demand for Rodial from mass stores that I couldn't sell to, I started thinking of creating a diffusion range that had some of the DNA of Rodial but was more affordable and was distributed through a different network. The formulas would need to be effective, but instead of having five active ingredients used in their maximum concentration we would focus on just one key ingredient that would do the job. I also recognised that this was a chance to target a slightly younger audience and focus on areas such as clogged and acne-prone skin, dehydration and first signs of ageing. I created a name that was inspired by the popular term for plastic surgery 'nip and tuck' and the catch-all, number-one fashion word, 'fabulous', and called the range NIP+FAB.

I had all the necessary internal resources by that time. Our design team put together the branding designs for NIP+FAB, we mocked up the range and presented it to the buyers rather than commit to a full production, as I had to do with Rodial. We first presented to Boots in the UK, who loved the concept and wanted to launch in 600 stores, and Target in the US, who wanted to launch in 1,000 stores. It was really exciting to get such a positive reaction to a new brand, especially after all the challenges I had when I was starting with Rodial. It did help, of course, that I had ten years of experience of running a very successful luxury skincare range and everyone knew about Rodial. It made my job so much easier.

Even though NIP+FAB started as a spinoff of Rodial, it very quickly developed its own identity and target market with innovative product and a very distinctive tone of voice. Over the years, NIP+FAB has revolutionised the market with skincare innovations in a whole range based on glycolic acid to combat acne, signs of ageing and uneven skin tone. It became one of the best-selling skincare ranges in mass market stores and pharmacies worldwide. NIP+FAB also revolutionised the market by introducing a treatment product in a pad format throughout all our ingredient ranges. The Glycolic Fix pads have become the best-selling pad product in all our retailers globally. Other ingredient ranges include Viper Venom, Dragon's Blood and Kale. We also developed a specialised body range for products to target cellulite and other tongue-in-cheek names such as Bust Fix, Tummy Fix and Upper Arm Fix. Our customers couldn't get enough!

Launching another range was a risk. Launching a range that could cannibalise our main range was an even bigger risk. But we went with it and NIP+FAB has grown over the years and has developed its own customer base very different to Rodial. The level of turnover will match that of Rodial in a few short years. It was a risk worth taking.

There comes a point, after you have been in business for a few years, that you need to create buzz on another level. I needed to take the next risk and the next challenge to grow my brand awareness and sales.

A very important part of growing a brand is keeping the interest of the public and the press. It is easy to capture the interest when you first start as the brand is new, exciting and has a different point of view. We worked very hard on the press during the first few years and it paid off. Press and in-store promotions were the main drivers of the sales. Yes, we did have some new products that got a bit of coverage but nothing too exciting. Over the years, the press would ask me if I would consider bringing a face of the brand on board and I used to always say no.

The NIP+FAB business grew fast and globally. We were soon available in more than 15,000 stores worldwide. Our biggest market was the US, having just launched in 8,000 stores. My sales teams were asking for some buzz in the US, and we needed to come up with something big …

Overnight Success Secret #6

The Importance of Taking Risks

Anyone can take risks even in their current job. Work extra hard. Offer to help outside your job description but don't just put yourself out there: make sure you learn some new skills. Don't be afraid to roll up your sleeves and show how committed and passionate you are about your job and your industry. Everywhere in life, people who succeed always take the extra step. I have seen this in my business, and the people who progressed from admin assistants to running departments always went out of the way to do more to deliver more. Not only were they rewarded within this business but they also learned skills that will help them to succeed in anything they choose to do with their lives and careers in the future.

You will never know the outcome of anything unless you take a risk. When I sent that handwritten letter to *Seventeen* magazine telling them what I thought the magazine was missing and that I would be the one to fill the gaps and bring them a breath of fresh air, I was exposing myself to rejection ... I could just have thought, 'They'll think I am an idiot, they will not even read my letter, I won't hear back for sure, why take the risk?' But I didn't ... or rather I did, but I ignored it. I had nothing to lose. When I decided not to continue with a career in finance and instead start my own business, I had no idea where this would lead me and I did have quite a lot to lose ... but if you don't do it you'll never know. The passion to at least TRY outweighed the fear of risk.

Whenever I am about to take a risk of any sort, I always calculate what is the worst thing that can happen. If I am able to live with the consequences of the worst-case scenario, I go for it. If you need to remortgage your house to start a business, I wouldn't take this lightly. It's a decision that takes a lot of thought. But if you hate your job or hate your industry but you are too comfortable where you are and you don't want to lose your high salary, do something about it now! Start researching the industry you want to get into, read industry-related books and publications, visit conferences, work out the ways you can lose that salary but still be happy. It's an equation . . . you need to calculate the pros and cons and weigh it up for yourself. And if the maths works then get updating your CV, get networking and get yourself out there! I had to go from a six-figure salary and dressing in Prada suits and bags every day to no salary for five years and running a business hand to mouth. No Prada for me – I was shopping at flea markets and on the high street. But that was what I needed to do to grow my business, that was a small sacrifice to be able to support my business and I was happy to dress on a budget when I had to.

Don't be afraid of things going wrong. At the beginning, everything that can go wrong WILL go wrong. And at the beginning when you start, you get more problems than you get victories. My first few years of running the business were all problems with people, products, cash flow – you name it, I went through it. And I always found a solution. In the early days, when we didn't have enough cash to pay the team and had to let people go, it was hard and heartbreaking but the business needed to survive. I had to make those hard decisions and it was a lot more difficult when there were only four people in the team. I still get problems of a different sort now, but having faced issues of 'Will the business survive another day?' made me a lot more thick-skinned and able take on problems in a calmer way.

And once you are in your dream job or have started your dream company, keep taking risks. Take risks to create buzz and be visible. Take risks to create something that stands out against the competition. Find ideas that will create buzz, get people talking and help your idea to go viral even when you have very little budget. I could have gone safe and called my product 'Anti-ageing Serum'. Boring. I went all the way and called it Snake Serum. The name created lots of free press, it went viral internationally and within a month of launching we were shipping pallets of Snake Serum all over the world. The things we regret in life are the things we don't do rather than the things we do. Time to take a risk.

7

Create
Buzz

When I started the business there were no funds for an office assistant, let alone for a PR agency. I was getting the Rodial name out there, but doing it on a shoestring. There were no Testino commissions or *Vogue* back-cover ads for us but it is possible to create buzz about your brand without a lot of money. You just need to think outside the box.

When we needed our first Rodial promotional postcard, there was no way we could afford a commercial printer, and besides they just laughed at the very idea of a print run of less than 10,000, so we just did everything at Vistaprint, using one of their template designs. Back then we did everything on paper, everything had to be printed out, artwork sent by post ... sometimes when I am on social media and I think back to how it was when I started it seems like another world, and I guess, in marketing terms, it was. When social media took off it was like we had suddenly discovered fire, or the wheel, or stretch denim ... nothing would ever be the same!

The key to creating buzz around your product is to get press and influencers talking about your brand. If you are just starting out in a new industry and you don't know who is who and you can afford to allocate some budget to a specialised PR agency, it is worth every penny. But do your research: make sure they are worth the investment. There are a lot of half-ass PR agencies out there and it can be hard to know who can do a good job and who is just going to take your money and then blame your product for not getting any press. Some are great in other fields but might be useless in your chosen industry ... some just might be useless. Ask for recommendations and get into a trial contract of three months to try things out and see how you get on. I have worked with a number of PR agencies over the years, large and small, and have seen everything.

When I started, I went with a large and reputable agency to establish the brand and also be in the company of other reputable brands. It's important that you feel you are getting your money's worth ... particularly if you don't have a lot of it and you do not want to be fobbed off. I have found that when the larger PR companies are pitching for your business you'll get the senior partners and creative directors come to see you ... but then six months down the line you find you are dealing with a junior account director and then the final ignominy ... you only get email replies from the intern.

With time, I decided to move to a smaller agency where our brands were the biggest and would get more attention. There are pros and cons to both. But just because you have a PR company working for you doesn't mean you let them get on with it. There is a clue in that last sentence; they are working for YOU! It can sometimes seem the other way around (it can be the same with model agencies and record companies) but remember you can hire and fire them, they are your employee (sort of), so make sure they are pulling their weight and doing things in the right way for your brand.

There were also times that I was tight with cash and had to manage PR internally and put a lot of personal work into it. Funnily enough, I would get twice the coverage. Plus any work you do is free (again ... sort of). It stands to reason that you know the industry and already know the players (magazines, onlines and bloggers) and it's just a matter of keeping those relationships alive, particularly if they are relationships you built yourself over the years so they would think of you and your brand every time they write something relevant. If you think the personal touch would be better than a blanket PR release to certain people, then you should do it.

I can't say, after working both with agencies and in-house, that one is necessarily better than the other as both options have their own challenges. If you have the time and the energy to develop those relationships, go for it and do it alone. But if PR is an afterthought and you wouldn't enjoy meeting and chasing journalists, then my advice is get a good PR agency to do the work for you.

The press are very spoilt for choice. They receive press releases on hundreds of new products per day and get calls from PRs about the latest, hottest new products. You need to have something new to talk about to the press all the time. You could be launching a new product every three months, like most beauty and fashion brands have to do now, or you can pitch about a trend related to your product. It's like finding a way to reinvent your product, giving it another spin. It could be a new use, a seasonal use or a new celebrity association.

It used to be that a product mention in *Vogue* magazine would get you tons of buzz and excitement and lots of sales. Of course, that hasn't completely changed … it is always exciting to see our products featured or recommended in the pages of a prestigious fashion or beauty magazine and it is still a huge boost for any brand (contrary to popular myth, the traditional print media isn't dead just yet), but it's even more important for your products to appear on social media; and when it comes to fashion and beauty, especially on Instagram. Bloggers and Instagrammers are creating trends and waiting lists, more so than the magazines. And let's not forget the vloggers and YouTubers – a whole new industry and a way of communicating with your end consumer that is direct and very real.

Another way to generate publicity is to work with a face of the brand. In the first years of building my business, I could barely afford to pay my staff's salaries, let alone pay for a face of the brand. But as you grow, there will be people out there who can bring some excitement into your brand without the need of huge amounts of investment. They don't need to be Hollywood stars but people within your market who have a high profile and could align with your brand.

Even though the landscape has changed, similar principles apply now as they did when I started the business. You put together an exciting press release about your product and start sending it to magazines. Now, you may ask yourself, why would they choose to feature your product as opposed to the competition? You need to grab their attention. The press release needs to be catchy, and the way you package and send the product needs to look beautiful and represent your brand. A handwritten note by the founder always helps. If you have a product that is different to the competition, you package it well and send it to the right people, it will be featured sooner rather than later. After sending it you need to follow up, but know your limits ... no one likes a stalker.

After a while of careful (non-stalking) communication, you will begin to develop personal relationships with your top journalists. Believe it or not, they are all people like you and will happily feature the brand or product of someone they like. But don't be fake. You must be really interested in them and be open and friendly but not pushy. It takes a while to build trust and you need to be genuine – you won't get along with everybody, that's just life, but be pleasant to them all the same ... it's a bit like a big family wedding, there are always a few in-laws you can't stand, but you want things to go smoothly so just smile and nod, smile and nod. Most of all, be yourself and you will find that there are journalists and bloggers out there who you get along with like best buddies. These are the relationships you should cherish.

The ultimate influencers that can help you create buzz are celebrities, of course. In a world that is dominated by the big brands who offer multi-million-dollar contracts to celebrities, how do you get your products in their hands and, better still, get them talking about it? Try to think about celebrities as normal people like you and me. Are you using products from just one brand in any area of your life? Don't you like to discover new and innovative products? It's the same with the celebrities. Even the ones with contracts with the big brands still like to discover and try new products. Many celebrities are locked into deals, it's true, but they may only have a contract with a hair brand, so if your product fits in a different category then there won't be a conflict for them and they may mention it in the press or on social media. Quite often, when celebrities are interviewed, they are asked by the publication to only mention a couple of products from the brand they endorse and the rest need to be from other brands, otherwise it starts to look less like an interview and more like an infomercial. If they use your products and they like them you may get lucky and, next time they give a press interview, they may mention them. I know there is a lot of 'may' and 'lucky' in there . . . but remember this is free advertising by a celebrity, which would cost you tens of thousands any other way. So, if you only get one mention from sending out 100 freebies then that is a solid win.

Sometimes, when posting on my @MrsRodial account or uploading to Instagram, it's easy to forget just how new all of this technology is. It has become part of everyday life so quickly that it really boggles me to think of a time (only five years ago!) when we didn't have it. When I started the business, it was a completely different world and working with an influencer was a very different process. Back in those ancient Before Instagram times, the influencers were traditional celebrities. As a small company with limited (i.e. zero) advertising budget, we would identify a celeb we thought went well with the brand, then send freebie products and goodie bags to their agent or publicist. We would then follow up by bombarding them with calls and emails to find out if the celeb in question had tried/liked/loved our products, and if they had, try to get an official quote. But that was only half the battle! If we did get a quote then phase two began: trying to convince fashion editors of various magazines and papers that it was worth printing. The bigger the name, the more likely we'd get some column inches ... such and such says 'Rodial changed my life' or 'All my Hollywood pals are getting Rodial for Christmas this year', etc. If we got the quote in a magazine then this hopefully would generate a lot of interest in the brand and sometimes sales too.

As the business gets more mature, you need to reinvent the brand (just like Madonna) and find ways to make your brand and products still relevant against the new brands cropping up everywhere. One way to do this is to host an event. It gives the press interesting content to cover. It does take more work and it's a bigger investment than a cup of coffee with a journalist, but it's worth it. Do it at a time when not much is happening in the social diary of your town. Everyone likes an invite and you would get both press and social media coverage. Especially if it's something as big as an awards show ...

Overnight Success Secret #7

Push Your Creative Limits

Are you pushing yourself and your business as far as you can? Sometimes pushing the limits means creating opportunities that other people don't see. If you look at the next five years, what are the things that you would like to achieve? Create the opportunities that will take you there in the next five years to ensure your business is at the forefront of innovation.

No matter how far you go with your current product or idea, you need to push the limits to keep your business fresh and current and relevant. You need to do everything it takes. It's not about beating competition, it's about becoming better than yourself. It's about pushing your limits every single day.

There are times when we are all stuck in a situation, and we feel there is nothing more we can offer. In business, you have to keep going. How do you get to push your limits every single day?

My ten tips to stay inspired and push your creativity:

1. It takes a lot of self-motivation to push your limits. Find a way to motivate yourself.
2. Browse on YouTube to find interviews with people you admire and watch them.
3. Change location. If you find yourself stuck to your desk and doing the same thing again and again, you need to change your energy. Visit a gallery or go to a place you have never been.

4. Cut pages from magazines of inspirational interviews with people you admire, and read them when you are feeling down.
5. Keep emails or notes thanking or praising you for something to read to boost your motivation.
6. Go to a bookstore and browse biographies, business books and inspirational stories.
7. Pick up the phone and speak to a friend for a light chat and a gossip.
8. Take time to spring clean your office or your wardrobe. It can be very cathartic and also clears your mind, ready for new goals.
9. Go for a run or walk in the park. Clear your head and new ideas will come flowing.
10. Have an espresso. It helps. No wonder it's called liquid ambition.

8

Awards, Glamour and Celebrities

Early in 2010, we wanted to celebrate ten years of Rodial and decided to do something different instead of another boring cocktail party. I thought, wouldn't it be fun to organise an awards event to celebrate all the women we love and have supported us over the years? I got very excited with the idea ... I have been a fan and follower of all kinds of award shows over the years, from the Oscars to the Glamour Woman of the Year and everything in between. However, the execution of an awards event for a tiny little beauty company sounded really huge and I honestly didn't believe we were at the level where we could pull it off. My PR team was pushing for the idea and left it open – they were willing to explore next steps and see where they would lead.

Well, I didn't put up too much of a fight because, in the few weeks following that meeting, we put together our very first 'Rodial Beautiful Awards' show. Held in the billiard room at London's Sanderson Hotel, it was small but stylish (like the brand!). So it was not quite on the scale of the Oscars or the Golden Globes, but we got a good deal for the space, and got drinks included, which was a bonus as we couldn't afford much at the time. We put a panel of judges together (mostly a combination of our friends) and sent them a list of nominees to pick from and, before I knew it, I was stood on stage and handing them out to the likes of Jade Jagger and Paloma Faith. That first year the awards ran very smoothly ... nobody fell up the steps, or sent an Apache Native American as a political protest or got Idina Menzel's name wrong. It was a great night, but more importantly the awards gave great visibility to Rodial; we got tons of press coverage, the right associations with celebrities and lots of content for PR and social media.

How did we secure the talent to attend the awards? Well, it worked like this. There were five categories of celebrities/VIPs: the panel, the presenters, the nominees and winners, and the VIP guests. The starting point was our judging panel who, as I mentioned, were mostly friends of the brand ... by getting them involved in the judging they felt like they had a bit of ownership of the awards themselves ... so we could rely on them to attend and most were happy to also present an award. To secure the rest was a combination of calling in favours on personal relationships with celebs and, if that didn't work, calling their agents. Dealing with agents is a delicate game ... and the key is finding a way to compromise. Generally, the equation goes something like this.

We would call Agent A and say we wanted to invite/give an award to Celebrity X (an A-list celebrity). Agent A would counter by suggesting Celebrities Y and Z (B- or C-list) in order to secure celebrity X or instead of Celebrity X. We would then call Agent B and say, 'Hey, Agent A is sending Celebrity X, Y and Z. I hear Celebrity X is good friends with your client Celebrity D [also A-List]. Would she like to present Celebrity X with their award? Yes, they will be on the top table ... yes, they will get a VIP goodie-bag ...' etc. Over the years, we have been lucky enough/clever enough to secure most of the A-list celebs we wanted as well as giving a chance (and a picture in *Grazia* or the *Evening Standard* magazine) to some wonderful up-and-coming talent as well, just to mix things up.

This was all going like clockwork and so by our third year we were on a roll. Agents and publicists were now calling us to get an invite or a guest presenter spot for their celebrity clients and we were now free to choose some really big names for our award nominees and be confident they would accept. Our award categories had settled into a familiar pattern by now as well and it had become established that one of the most prestigious awards of the evening was for 'Classic Beauty'. The award winner was always an established model or actress with classic looks and impeccable style. The first couple of years the award had been given to Jade Jagger and Paloma Faith. This year, the vote had been a tie between Yasmin Le Bon and Elle Macpherson, but we did not want to weaken the accolade by making them share it. Instead, we saw this as a great opportunity to create a special new award, 'Woman of the Year', to give to Elle to acknowledge all she had achieved in the beauty and fashion industries, while Yasmin would be the worthy sole winner of the 'Classic Beauty' award.

Well, Elle and Yasmin are both huge names in fashion. They both confirmed attending through their agents ... but we've heard that story before. One of the biggest challenges when putting together the Rodial Beautiful Awards was the last-minute cancellations of winners. This was to be expected – all events experience cancellations on the day – but it creates a ripple of issues through other factors related to the event. For example, if a winner cancels, the presenter of the award needs to be briefed last minute to change the wording of their intro, with a suitable 'I'm afraid they can't be with us tonight as they are shooting a new campaign in blah-blah' or 'They have sent us this message ...' As a result, the award announcement runs smoothly and it looks like we knew all along that we would have to find someone relatable to the winner to accept on their behalf. It can be quite a scramble but, as I have learned, it's all part and parcel of the business of awards.

So, having experienced this before, and with my natural cautiousness, I was worried whether either Yasmin Le Bon or Elle Macpherson would cancel, but hopefully not both. Thankfully, both of them made it and each got their own award, giving the most graceful acceptance speeches.

I will always remember the moment when Elle accepted her award and made a beautiful speech talking about how she was thrilled to be recognised at that stage of her career and that she was pleased to be part of an evening that was all about women who were inspiring others and running successful businesses.

Year four was the most stressful of all. After the success of the category for Elle the previous year, we reintroduced it for the next year and the panel vote for Woman of the Year went to Kate Moss. I got straight on to her agent to confirm that she would be attending to receive her award. The agent said that unfortunately she wouldn't attend. To be fair, it wasn't just about diaries: I would have been surprised if she did attend as she was under contract to Rimmel and showing up at our event to get a Rodial award would probably be a breach of contract. However, one of my people at work claimed that they were best buddies with Kate and she would definitely attend the awards. I was sceptical, but this was someone I trusted … She said that she was in touch with her directly: 'In fact, stop talking to the agent, I'm best friends with Kate and she has told me she is definitely going to be there.' OK, why should I doubt my employee?

Yes, you've guessed it. The evening started and Kate was nowhere to be seen. I should have gone with my instincts … and more importantly with my experience. Luckily, my experience also meant we could save it. I knew that James Brown, Kate's hairdresser, was there and he agreed to pick up the award for her. It was all seamless, apart from the heightened stress levels, of course.

The fifth Rodial Beautiful Awards were the best ever. By that time, we had moved the location for the awards to a larger space on Saint Martin's Lane, turned it into a sit-down dinner, appointed Laura Whitmore as a presenter and even hired Sean Canning, one of the UK's most renowned awards scriptwriters, to put together the script for the whole evening. By now, the Rodial Awards had become a firm fixture on the beauty and fashion industry calendar and we had connections with all the major agents. Every January we would start getting calls asking when the awards were happening so they could suggest which of their clients would be available and push for invites of new ones. There is always a new movie, a new campaign or a new album to sell and celebrities need to be seen at the right events with the right crowd (such as the Rodial Beautiful Awards – ahem). They are the perfect opportunity to boost a celebrity profile.

By year five we were saying 'No' more often than 'Yes' to guest-list additions and the Rodial Beautiful Awards had developed a reputation as one of the most glamorous and sophisticated events in London. Our international PR agencies wanted to take the awards to NY, LA, Europe and Asia, so we were on to something!

There are so many elements that go into creating an event of such a size. From the production and build, to scripts and running of the show, to menu choices, music, live performances, guest-list management, seating, VIP seeding and panel selection. Everyone wants to be invited – friends of friends of friends – which can make it tough to accommodate everyone, leaving some people unhappy. We'd have people who had attended the awards one year, but had not made the guest list the next ...

Another issue we faced, which I hadn't anticipated, was the reaction of some nominees who got very upset that they did not win their categories ... especially bloggers. At one awards, when we announced the winner of the beauty blogger category, a nominee stormed out of the awards, evidently presuming she was going to win ... and then immediately unfollowed us on social media. Others would express their disappointment publicly on Twitter and diss the awards. What is it with bloggers? You know that moment at the Oscars where the screen splits into four as they announce the winner and the three losers all graciously applaud? I would love to have seen that screen during our blogger category ... it would have been far more entertaining. Anyhow, by year five we had endured enough and we decided not to include any bloggers in our categories ... they were taking everything way too personally and posting all their bile online so it was a lose/lose situation for us.

Another category that we dropped was for the makeup artists. This was another category that created resentment if the nominees didn't win (although they weren't as bad as the bloggers) and as we work with a lot of makeup artists as a brand we were making fewer friends and more enemies.

The awards in 2014 were our last. By that time we had raised the brand awareness but felt that it had all become a bit of a publicity game: it just didn't feel right any more. As it was the best year ever, it was a good way to bow out.

Another element of hosting the awards was that I got to connect with existing celebrity fans of the brands or make new ones.

I met Daisy Lowe at the 5th Rodial Beautiful Awards. She won the ultimate award that year, the Woman of the Year. She was part of that London IT crowd, the 20-something group including Alexa Chung and Cara Delevingne that looked effortless and fashionable, and everyone wanted a piece of them. Daisy was very sweet at the awards and we immediately hit it off! She sent me a bouquet of beautiful flowers the day afterwards with a note, and I thought how charming. I then bumped into her a few times in the next few months and loved her energy and effortless style.

It was May 2014 and we were planning our autumn campaign to launch our new sculpting and contouring makeup range. I wanted to make a statement, to make everyone pay attention to our makeup as if it was a new range, rather than an extension of our existing skincare. What do the big brands do when they want to make a statement? They hire a celebrity and make her the face of the brand.

With every success there is always added pressure to deliver. And we needed to deliver on creating buzz around makeup. It wasn't going to be just sending some powders and mascaras over to the press. We needed something bigger ...

I was at the office and brainstorming with my Marketing and PR team. What shall we do, how do we make a statement? We started discussing bringing in a celebrity. We were just starting out a campaign with Milly Mackintosh for NIP+FAB and we didn't yet have any results on press or sales to justify making another investment, but we didn't have the time to wait. The results of the Milly campaign would be known by October and the makeup was launching early November. The planning of a campaign shoot takes a month, then another few weeks to select and get the pictures ready, and you need to present to the press three months before the launch to catch the long lead time of monthly magazines. We needed to make a decision there and then and take that risk if we were to make the deadlines.

We talked about a few options. We decided to focus on a UK personality as makeup was initially launching in the UK – it wouldn't be launched in the US for another year. This already narrowed it down to a few people: Alexa Chung, Kate Moss, Rosie Huntington-Whiteley and Daisy

Lowe. Alexa was already working with a few beauty brands, Kate was still with Rimmel and Rosie was all over the press with Marks & Spencer. Also, I always like to know all the personalities with whom we work and, having met and liked Daisy, I thought she would make an excellent choice.

When you want to work with a personality you deal with their agent or manager. You negotiate everything from the duration of the contract to the number of days they will represent the brand (shoot, press interviews and appearances), hair and makeup budget, travel arrangements, even the number of days within which the talent has to approve the pictures (the brand wants the pictures ASAP and the personality always tries to negotiate as much time as they can to approve these).

My PR team worked with her manager to agree on the details. We started negotiations during the summer and it was challenging with all of us being away at different times, so by September we still didn't have a signed contract in place! While we were dealing with the legal elements of the agreement, we were also planning the photoshoot for mid-October. We booked the photographer and a stylist, and brought in everyone at our offices to discuss mood and style. I cut out some pages from French *Vogue* of a really cool shoot I liked that was very moody and the clothes were edgy with a French twist. The team was ready to go and we would shoot at the Worx studios in Parsons Green, London. We would shoot Daisy with two different looks, a day and an evening sculpt, and four different outfits.

It was now a week before the shoot and we still hadn't signed the contract. There were a few details that we thought were minor but they weren't to the other party and the negotiations dragged on for much longer than we thought. A few days before the shoot, I was invited to a fashion party and I bumped into Daisy and her manager. Things were a bit tense as we were all ready to go but no contract was signed. We had a quick chat and I reassured them that it was going to happen and I was looking forward to working with Daisy. Sometimes lawyers tend to complicate things and this was the situation. I felt we cleared the air with that conversation. The next day the contract was signed by both parties.

The day of the shoot arrived. At Worx, everyone was very excited but stressed as not only were we shooting a personality, we were also shooting makeup looks with our new makeup. Every look had to work with the hair and the outfit, and if not coordinated this could be a disaster. What I love about shoots these days is that there is a laptop where the pictures immediately load and you can see exactly what is being shot and what the pictures look like. The pictures looked great!

As part of our contract with Daisy, we had agreed to develop a limited edition glamstick (a high pigmented lip butter with a tint) with the name 'Just Daisy'. We wanted to launch the product in January 2015 for the second quarter of Daisy's contract with us. If we could dictate the timing, we would have ordered the product in August, giving us time for the press samples to be ready in October and the finished product ready for the stores in January. Because we didn't have a contract with Daisy until October but we needed to have a product ready, we looked at some of her press pictures and developed a colour that looked like the sort that she would wear. We placed the order in August.

On the day of the shoot, my product development manager came to me, very excited, holding a glamstick in her hands. It was the brand new Just Daisy glamstick! The timing couldn't have been better. She took the glamstick to Daisy. Daisy took my PR aside to talk.

I could sense something was wrong. Daisy didn't like her lipstick colour and thought it didn't represent her. I had a look at the colour myself and, I have to say, it was supposed to be a reddish coral and was more of a dirty orange. It wasn't great. I immediately called the office to see what was the situation. We had approved the colour but at times there is a slight difference in the final product. Well, we need to change this, my team said. We had only produced the press products, which were a couple of hundred – so no big deal, we can redo the whole production in a new colour. There was silence … My product manager said, 'We have a problem. As it was a limited edition, the factory ran the whole 5,000 pieces and we now have the entire stock in our warehouse!'

I couldn't believe it. I was taking risks every day with my business and this was a risk that just hadn't paid off. I had 5k units of glamstick that I couldn't sell! Okay, fine … breathe, think. For starters, let's get a new colour and get our 'Just Daisy' made right, then we can deal with this stock. It wasn't just that we had to bin 5,000 items, we also needed to move fast to get a new version ready for January. We had a disaster on our hands. The team worked closely with Daisy to develop a colour that she liked and we nailed it within a week and produced the entire run within three months. Which wasn't quite January … it was February by the time we got everything done, but it wasn't the show-stopper we feared. It was still done in time to be within contract. What did we do with the 5k overstock? We removed the Just Daisy labels and gave it away as gratis to our stores and staff. I never want to waste product.

A week after the campaign shoot, we selected the pictures and invited the press for interviews. Daisy and I took over the library at the Soho Hotel. We had all the top beauty editors including those at *Grazia* and *InStyle* magazine, and Daisy talked about her beauty routine while I spoke about why I picked her to be the face of our new makeup range and what the range was all about. It was all very fun and informal and a great day! Each journalist selected the pictures they liked for their feature, and articles started coming out in a few weeks. It was all really exciting as we were getting press both for our makeup and about Daisy being the face of our launch campaign.

Among the key products of the campaign were our luxury powders – packed in to-die-for compacts. The compacts incorporated textured vegan leather and shiny silver hardware and our big 'R' for Rodial. The compacts looked stunning and they are now the hero product of our makeup range. The powders themselves (contouring, bronzing, highlighting and perfecting in a variety of shades) have become some of our best-selling items, and are consistently featured in magazines and winning awards. They are loved by celebrity makeup artists worldwide and used by the likes of Mario Dedivanovic on Kim Kardashian and it's a staple of his masterclasses. Val Garland uses it on the models when she is creating catwalk looks for the various fashion shows.

Through the awards and celebrity associations, we were able to get the word out about our products to a different market that doesn't follow the beauty pages and now became aware of our brand and products.

Overnight Success Secret #8

How to Organise a Successful PR Event

There is nothing like holding a successful PR event to generate buzz about your business. Over the years, I have organised all sorts of events, from PR breakfasts to bloggers cocktail parties to VIP dinners to masterclasses. You put a lot of time, energy and money into these events but if you do them right the buzz that you get is totally worth it.

These are my top ten tips for organising a buzzworthy event:

1. Find a reason for the event. It could be anything from launching a new product to celebrating a business anniversary, a holiday or season of the year or even a collaboration. It's not hard to find a reason but you really need one to throw an event.
2. Be very clear at the beginning what do you want to achieve: to get press coverage for your product, introduce your product to influencers, get coverage in the social pages or get tagged on lots of Instagram pictures. Write down what your goals are so you can plan accordingly.
3. Decide on the number of people and the type of event. Think about people's schedules and the likelihood they would attend an event. Breakfasts and drinks are the easiest as people can go before or after work. I find lunches to be the most challenging. In the time it takes to travel to the

venue, drinks, then sit down to a two- or three-course meal and then make your way back, that's half the day gone. If your target market is 'ladies who lunch' then you'd be spot on.

4. Find a venue that suits the style of your brand. If you have a cool, edgy brand, you want a venue that represents it and nothing too corporate or traditional. It's all in the details. People always like to go to a new venue, so if there's something new and exciting and it fits your brand and your budget, go for it.

5. During the first few years of the business we organised all the events with an internal team. We still organise some of the more intimate events ourselves. We just ensure we have enough 'pairs of hands' for the event and we enlist the help of people outside the PR team to help. Other staff are all excited to be part of an event and you get a lot of volunteers. Make sure everyone knows their exact job when they are there. Allocate roles in advance.

6. Branding of the venue is important. It has to look like your event. Anything from a welcome poster on arrival, branded goodie bags and products thrown around the space are easy ways to dress a room. Mix it up with some flowers and you are good to go.

7. Don't forget to remind your guests of your social media handles and general hashtags as well as any special hashtag for the evening. You need all the social media support you can get!

8. A step-and-repeat (a wide wall where your logo is repeated, as shown at red-carpet events) is a

great way to get some branding into the room and ensure that your logo is in photographs. If the space allows, your guests will feel like they are walking the red carpet! And that means more pictures and social media impressions.

9. These days we use e-vites from most of our events but it is always a nice touch if you send a handwritten note to some of your top guests. If you want to send an invitation card, then go for something really special, using an unusual paper finish, colour or material to make an impact. Oversize invites are always fabulous.

10. Enjoy the time! This is easier said than done. I always tend to worry at my events – Will my guests show up? Will they have a good time? etc. I am becoming better at this but I still tell myself to relax and enjoy.

9 The Kardashian Factor

I was never a fan of the *Keeping up with the Kardashians* show. I have watched a few scenes over the years while switching channels but I never watched an entire episode from start to finish. That doesn't mean it's bad ... I'm just more of a *House of Cards* gal, that's all. I knew about the family through the various media stories that surfaced and was always impressed at how they worked social media, Twitter and then Instagram to become the first Insta-famous personalities with thousands of selfies and millions of followers.

Over the last couple of years, I started noticing the two younger sisters, Kendall and Kylie Jenner. They had followed a similar route to fame as the rest of the Kardashian clan: exposure on the TV show followed by a masterful social media presence, and they too had begun to build a career for themselves outside of the show. I'd seen Kendall walk at the Chanel shows and her younger sister Kylie endorse a hair range; I saw them in *Time* magazine among the 'Most Influential Teens of 2014'; and the more I saw, the more I thought that there was something really cool about them. So, I joined millions of others who obviously felt the same and started following them on Instagram ... and, apart from liking the odd selfie, that, as far as I was aware at the time, was that.

Months later in 2014 I was casually flicking through Instagram posts and there was Kylie at a shoot in LA ... and what had she posted? Only a picture of the NIP+FAB Glycolic Fix! Woo-hoo! This was brilliant! Over the years we have gifted makeup artists with both Rodial and NIP+FAB products, so it wasn't unusual for them to show up at a shoot, and we quite frequently get unexpected feedback that a certain celebrity has used one of our products and become a big fan. Sometimes we hear about it, sometimes we don't ... but it's always a thrill when we do.

Now, there a couple of reasons why she may have posted the product pic: it may be that she absolutely loved the product and couldn't wait to tell the world (this is my preferred scenario) or it could be that she just needed material for her daily feed ... either way this was an amazing piece of exposure for our brand. At the time NIP+FAB was a relatively unknown brand in the US and Kylie had just Instagrammed us to her 22 million followers, which in turn led to over half a million likes.

Needless to say, after pausing to do a little dance around the kitchen, I immediately reposted it on our own social media. That one post was the beginning of a very exciting journey between Kylie and NIP+FAB.

The result of the post was not just a lot of interest on our own @nipandfab handle but also for our brand in general. The calls and email traffic we got from people wanting to find out more about our products went up dramatically, and this pushed the button on something I'd been thinking about for a while, namely using 'influencers' to help enhance the brand. The internal debate had gone back and forth a few times on whether it would be best to go with a 'traditional' celebrity (model, film star, singer, etc.) or align with a purely digital talent like Zoella (millions of followers, zeitgeist, etc.). Here, all of sudden, was Kylie Jenner ... seemingly the best of both worlds!

We looked at Kylie and the effect that single Instagram had on our brand and I decided to take things to the next level. We got in touch with her agent in December 2014 and started talks. I wanted to work with her as an official N+F brand ambassador. We would build a whole event around the announcement; we'd bring her to London to meet her fans and do a series of press and social events to celebrate her association with the brand.

The negotiations took four nail-biting months, and there were many times that I thought the deal wouldn't go through at all. Dates went back and forth – she was busy filming her show, and, as you might expect for one of the most influential people of 2014, she had a few other engagements to attend – so trying to slot it all in was proving very difficult. In the meantime, while the negotiations around Kylie swirled, we had the practical business of planning an event, which, if we left it too late, would cause us even more problems, so we were looking at venues, booking hotels, planning parties … all the while not quite sure whether it was actually going to happen. Every day for the whole four months I would be on the phone until late in the evening with my team getting updates from the negotiations with team Jenner in LA.

Finally, we picked Westfield in Shepherd's Bush, West London, as our key photo call and consumer venue. This is a luxury shopping centre that combines a selection of massive flagships stores for Prada, Louis Vuitton and Burberry with a great selection of high-street stores, restaurants and cinemas. It is well known, suits the brand and was available on the dates that Kylie wanted. The venue was booked. Everything was in place for 14 March 2015 for our 24 hours with Kylie in London.

Well, not quite. During our negotiations with venues and hotels we had played our cards very close to our chests … we didn't want news of NIP+FAB's new brand ambassador getting leaked so we hadn't told Westfield who our celebrity was going to be. 'Loose lips sink ships,' as they say. We had mentioned it would be a 'big name' and we'd let them know that security would be needed. They've had a lot of A-list names at Westfield in the past so this was well within their normal event protocol.

With a week to go we had a final production meeting at Westfield with their event manager and security. We started to talk about cars and escorting the talent to the stage and so forth, and thought it only polite to tell them who they should be looking out for. 'It's Kylie Jenner,' I said proudly. There was an uncomfortable silence. 'You know ... from the Kardashians.' I smiled for extra emphasis but this last bit seemed to make the atmosphere even more tense.

Finally, the event manager spoke: 'The Kardashian family are banned from Westfield, I'm afraid.'

Kill me now.

Hmm, yes, so it seems I missed the headlines in November 2012 when Kim, Khloé and Kourtney launched their Dorothy Perkins fashion collaboration with Philip Green. They'd planned a signing in the main event space and the event had turned to chaos as thousands of teenage fans, having queued through the night, broke through police barriers and mobbed the malls ... several casualties and fainting teens later Westfield had called time on having any more Kardashian-related events at the centre.

I had to save the NIP+FAB event ... too many wheels were already in motion. We were running a competition for customers to come along and be a VIP, the press had been sent 'save the date' invites: this event had to stay on the rails. I guess they sensed my desperation. OK, they agreed, the event could go ahead but you are going to need to triple the security, we need to inform the police, we need ambulances on standby ... the list went on, and the bill went up. I simply could not afford to spend that much money. We kept talking.

The problem with the 2012 event was that it was public, with lots of promotion, lots of pre-event press and held in the main event space in the centre of the mall. Although this space was exactly where we were proposing the big reveal of our NIP+FAB star, the difference was that we hadn't actually announced it yet ... could we make this a secret, exclusive event?

Well, the public event space was out of the question now. The events manager suggested we might hold it in one of their onsite cinemas. It would be a theatre setting and we could get Kylie to and from the stage without having to walk her through the shopping centre. It'd be different, more low-key, but yes, it could work. However, we still needed to announce that it would be Kylie Jenner and tell people and press where to come. The potential that this could go viral and send thousands of Kylie Jenner fans descending on Westfield was still a problem. We decided that we would release the news that our N+F ambassador would be Kylie but keep the venue secret until the last minute. After all, to make this worthwhile we still needed to create a buzz with this event .... if it was just Kylie and I sat in a room looking at each other it wasn't going to get a lot of press.

We officially announced the '24 Hours in London with Kylie Jenner' event and the press began to heat up. Meanwhile, it was all hands on deck to ensure everything was perfect. We had booked her and her team a suite at the Edition hotel and my team swapped out the hotel toiletries and decked it out with NIP+FAB products. From NIP+FAB shower gels and body creams, to face cleansers and serums, along with a beautiful Smythson washbag monogrammed with her initials. I wrote a note to her and left it in her room: 'Dear Kylie, welcome to London. I look forward to our 24 Hours together, let's rock it! XMaria'.

All week, right up until the moment she got on board that BA flight from LA to London, I still wasn't sure this would go through. I had been living on the edge for four months, I'd put a lot of resources into this project as well as all my energy and needed this to be a success. It was a big risk.

With 24 hours to go we sent out the 'secret location' details to the press, beauty-industry VIPs and our competition winners. I was enjoying the cloak and dagger ... it reminded me of the secret warehouse raves I'd gone to as a student, waiting in a bar for the text to tell you where the party was. You felt 'in the know' and special. Maybe this was better than the original concept.

Kylie arrived on a Friday and went straight to the Edition hotel. Paparazzi were waiting for her at the airport and, before I even got to meet her, a Mail Online story came up with her pictures at the airport talking about her trip to London as the brand ambassador for NIP+FAB. OK, this is working! She arrived with her manager Liz and her hair and makeup artist Rob Scheppy, who joined them from Paris after spending a week taking care of Kylie's sister Kim Kardashian and her newly dyed platinum hair. We were in constant communication with Liz. Kylie wanted to do some sightseeing in London and we organised for her to visit the London Eye.

My team and I went to the Edition hotel to pick her up and, although we had spoken on the phone, this was the first time I had actually met her. Her hair and makeup were immaculate, and she was dressed in high thigh boots and a satin top. We were at the same height with me wearing my double-decker Alaia boots. Between her people and mine there were about ten of us, and the moment we got out of the cars at the London Eye we were surrounded by a throng of paparazzi. Kylie and her team picked up the pace to outrun the paps ... but my double-decker Alaia boots had other ideas. No way was I running anywhere! The swarming paparazzi were there at every turn but we had a lovely afternoon, and finally, after a dinner at Nobu, we all had an early night. Tomorrow was going to be a big day.

We started with a photo shoot of Kylie at the Edition hotel for pictures that we would use to promote her role as the brand ambassador for NIP+FAB. She was ready to go at 9am sharp, hair and makeup done and not a sign that she hadn't slept all night because of the jet lag. We were also filming the segment so we could make clips for our social media accounts and YouTube. The shoot went very smoothly apart from the moment we looked around and realised we had lost Rob Scheppy. The room was big but not that big. Luckily we found him quickly enough!

The next part of the day was like a blizzard. We both headed off in limos with our teams and made our way to Westfield. Men in black suits talking into their sleeves directed us through the back of the mall where we disembarked and headed into a labyrinth of tunnels. I swear, if any of us had taken a wrong turn I'm pretty sure we'd still be down there now. Finally, we emerged, probably through a secret Scooby-Doo-style bookcase, I don't really recall, into the VIP lounge of the cinema. Time for another photo call, and this was where the first real step of Kylie's engagement with the brand would happen. We briefly went into the green room (a separate area with drinks and sofas where we could prep and wait until we were ready to hit the photo call). Then we stepped out to walk the red carpet (actually, not red but 'NIP+FAB blue' for the occasion) and face the press pit ... I couldn't believe it ... there must have been 100 photographers lined up, camera flashes strobing wildly, TV crews shouting our names for interviews and quotes. It was insane. I couldn't believe I was part of this. I looked at Kylie and was struck by how completely composed and in control she seemed, and then it hit me – of course she would be, this sort of attention and intensity is part of her everyday life. To me, it all seemed like a dream.

In the cinema, we stepped up on to the stage for a live Q&A to warm applause and more than a few screams and whoops. As well as inviting the press, we had given away 200 tickets to NIP+FAB customers and Kylie fans through our website and social media, and it looked like our 'last-minute reveal' of the location had worked because they were all here! Our host for the interview was the fabulous MTV presenter Becca Dudley, and we spoke about why we picked Kylie as the brand ambassador of NIP+FAB. Kylie talked about her favourite beauty products and style tips. The packed auditorium hung on our every word. I hoped I was making sense as I answered the questions as I was very nervous and all I could think was 'Let's just get through this.'

The Q&A flashed by and before I knew it Becca was thanking the audience and it was all over. We headed back to the Edition restaurant for lunch with Kylie and her manager, finally free of constant attention from press and photographers; it was the first quiet moment that we had together. Batteries recharged, we headed right back into the fray with interviews and filming with *Grazia* and *People* magazines, and a lovely end to the day at a tea party co-hosted by *InStyle* magazine. Kylie and I took some pictures in our fun photo booth and I was very happy to wrap up the day.

The press and social media went crazy with all the content. It was a lot of planning and hard work but definitely worth it. The products that Kylie promoted on the day were the NIP+FAB Glycolic Pads and the newly launched NIP+FAB Dragon's Blood range. The products flew off the shelves and are still on our best-selling list.

Things don't always work out when you want to bring celebrities in to help promote your brand. With NIP+FAB doing well, we started to think about bringing in someone a bit more mature (mind you, 'mature' in the model world is not what mature is to the real world) to associate with the brand and help us capture a different audience. Ideally, it would be someone who'd be recognisable both in the UK and the US with a good sense of style and that the media and our fans would be interested in and able to relate to.

We came up with the name of a model in her early 30s, who was a new mum and based in LA. We all got very excited. My team immediately got in touch with the people at her agency and started the negotiations. We would make her a brand ambassador for NIP+FAB, we'd launch her involvement with a campaign shoot in LA, press interviews, a launch event with step-and-repeat boards, the whole lot. We went back and forth on the phone and by email for a month and finally secured a date. So far so good. These negotiations always take a lot of time, but we had pretty much everything agreed when we booked our flights to LA for the first round of PR activity with her. We were now ten days out from the shoot and had a couple of details to finalise with her agency. My team kept emailing them but suddenly they weren't responding. That was a bit odd, and we still needed to sign the contract … but still, this was not that unusual. When we worked with Kylie Jenner, we had finalised the contract a couple of days before, and it all ran on rails. So I guess her agent is busy, not a biggie. We'll sort it nearer the time.

A few days before we are scheduled to leave for LA, I wake up and as always the first thing I do is check my Instagram feed. I'm scrolling down, checking on last night's posts, liking this and that …. and what do I see? It's an Instagram post from our soon-to-be NIP+FAB ambassador, promoting a competing skincare brand and saying how much she loves their products – wait, what? We are a week before entering into a long-term ambassadorial contract and she is announcing that she is doing digital work for the competition? It was 6am in the morning and my WhatsApp was burning up with the messages firing between me and my team, who were as shocked as I was to wake up to this.

Still stabbing away at WhatsApp, I made my way to the office and called an emergency meeting with my team. Well, I didn't need to call it … they were all there ready to fight the fire! What on earth do we do now? Here was the new brand ambassador who, in our eyes, had pulled the rug from under our whole campaign. Well, thanks to her agency being completely incommunicado for the past week we still hadn't signed the contract – not our fault, we had been ready and willing – but it meant that legally we could get out of this.

Every relationship we cultivate with our brand ambassadors has to be based, like any relationship in fact, on trust, compatibility and mutual respect. I felt that we had been 'dissed'. Even if we were out of contract, posting something like that a week before our campaign may be legally OK but it was morally dubious for sure. It ruined the integrity of the message (i.e. our newly appointed celebrity ambassador likes OUR brand best!). There was no way we could face the press and tell that story of how she was representing NIP+FAB when a few days before she was endorsing a competing skincare brand. We had already spent a lot of money on this campaign … flights, hotels, bookings at studios and so on … but, even worse, we had booked interviews and exclusives press calls, and all manner of PR relationships were now at stake. Despite all this, the feeling in the room was unanimous. We decided to pull the deal and face the consequences.

Looking back, it was absolutely the right thing to do. We stood by our values and this partnership just wasn't meant to be. We let the press know, we got over it and we moved forward. No regrets.

Overnight Success Secret #9

Influence the Influencers

The key to creating buzz around your product is to get press and influencers talking about your brand. You need to get your products into the pages of the most prestigious magazines, but without paying for high-price advertising. And these days it's even more important to get bloggers, vloggers and Instagrammers talking about your products to create a sense of excitement and buzz. One of the best ways of influencing the influencers is to get your products into the hands of celebrities without having to pay. These are my top ten steps:

1. Identify the celebrities that you want to approach.
2. Do some research and find out if they currently have any live contracts with big brands and, if so, in what category.
3. Narrow it down to celebrities who don't have competing contracts with your category.
4. Find out the names and addresses of their agents and publicists.
5. Send two sets of products, one for the agent/publicist and one for the celebrity.
6. Write a handwritten note on a beautiful card and be nice but not pushy.
7. Follow up with an email a week later to find out if the agent/publicist received the products and what they thought of them.

8. If you are lucky you may get a thank you, from the publicist, that such and such a celeb has received your products; if you are even luckier you may receive a thank-you note from the celebrity themselves.
9. Stop communication or else this may backfire and the agent/publicist think you are a pushy weirdo.
10. When you have a new product, repeat the process.

10

Becoming
Insta-
Famous

It's hard to remember life before social media. I joined the social media game very late. I was the last of my friends to get on Facebook and I rarely used it. I am very private when it comes to my personal life and didn't see the point of sharing stuff with non-friends ... or for that matter with friends who already knew what I was doing as I actually spoke to them. I was married and wasn't looking for love and I didn't particularly feel I needed any new friends, I had enough already and, with my hectic work schedule, I had barely any time to connect with the ones I did have. I didn't get why people would post endless (and usually bad-quality) pictures of themselves, their families and their friends partying or on holiday, and have other people comment on it. Still, everyone was doing it so I reluctantly signed up on Facebook but never went on it or checked it. I would, however, use it for work to announce a new launch, a new store, a new press success and so on.

In the autumn of 2011, I came across Twitter for the first time. In case you are reading this in some alternative dimension or dystopian future where Twitter no longer exists ... hard to believe but you never know ... Twitter is an online social networking service that enables users to send and read short messages called 'tweets'. It was created in March 2006 and quickly gained worldwide popularity. As of September 2016, Twitter had 695 million users, out of which more than 342 million were active users. I loved the fact that at the time you could post only 140 characters – it's succinct and you can run a commentary without the need of images or preparation. I also loved the fact that the following doesn't need to be reciprocal. You follow who you want and vice versa.

I had been reading about Twitter for a few months and on 30 December 2012, I set up my first Twitter account and made it my New Year's resolution to make it big over the next year. I needed to pick a name. My last name is lengthy, difficult to pronounce and almost always gets misspelled. I wanted something simple and easy and something that reflects who I am. And came up with the handle @MrsRodial. How do you start? I started following magazines, press, bloggers and friends in the hope that they would follow me back and would move from the embarrassing three followers I started with to a few hundred and then to a few thousand and so on. As far as content was concerned, I was in NY with my family at the time and it was Christmas so I had plenty of material to report on, from visits to the Met, to lunch at Cipriani, to a viewing of *Spider-Man: Turn Off the Dark* on Broadway. It was really fun and I was excited to have found a social media platform that I enjoyed.

From day one, I decided to keep my own account personal, and while reporting on my day-to-day life, trips, press events, celebrity friends, I wouldn't go big on promoting products unless there was something really important to me that I needed to share, like a favourite product or a beauty tip. I also loved posting inspirational messages. Sometimes, by posting those messages, I was motivating myself first and then my followers.

When I was back from NY in the New Year, I asked my team to set up Twitter accounts for our brands: @rodialskincare and @nipandfab. The question was who would run those accounts? Our PR department was the perfect platform as it was dealing daily with product launches, events, celebrity endorsements and generally all the exciting and glamorous stuff that was happening in our business. We needed to find a tone of voice that would be relevant to each brand. Rodial was more sophisticated, grown up and luxury, while NIP+FAB was younger, trendier and more informal, but they would both be run by one department. Apart from my early Luddite attitude to a personal Facebook account, I quickly learned to take social media very seriously ... today, it is how the brand is represented to the outside world and I need to be on top of it. You can't get an intern and let them run with it ... it would be a repeat of my first design agency commission. I know what is right for the brand so I give the overall tone and direction of our social media and my team executes. I have heard plenty of cautionary stories over the years of PR assistants live tweeting from a club on a Saturday night to the horror of the followers and their bosses. So I needed to be in control. I'm not saying my PR team are wild party animals ... but y'know, better safe than sorry.

There was so much we could share with our followers, it was really exciting to have this platform of communication. For our Rodial Beautiful Awards, we tweeted everything from the names of the celebrity nominees, to what the celebrity arrivals were wearing on the night of the awards, to who won! And when our celebrity fans tweeted about a Rodial product they loved, we would retweet that to share with our audience.

However, when we first started this was a completely new form of communication ... somehow I had to learn all about it. No one from PR had dealt with it before, there were no 'social media experts' back then, so I did what I always do when I face the unknown. I ordered a bunch of books from Amazon (*How to Tweet, Tweeting for Dummies,* etc. – you get the idea) and read them over a weekend. I summarised what I read, trailed a few things out on my own @mrsrodial account and sat down with my PR team on a Monday morning and took them through the do's and don'ts. I was monitoring the feed daily and gave back feedback. Another way to find out how to tweet, as with everything in life, is to watch how other people are doing it. When you first start tweeting, it does feel a bit awkward and forced but the more you do it the easier it becomes, and the less you worry about it the more naturally it comes across.

While the @rodialskincare and @nipandfab accounts were run by our PR department with my input, I would run my @mrsrodial account 100 per cent myself.

I have to admit that I became obsessed with Twitter. I would vent if I had a problem that day or talk about something I was proud of, and my followers mostly responded positively. I did have the occasional negative comment but that's social media. I was checking my timeline every hour and posting a few times a day, including early mornings, evenings after work and weekends. Twitter became part of my life and I loved it. I then noticed that people were live tweeting during popular TV shows and I loved that. I was looking forward to watching a show not just because of the show but for the comments I would share with other people on Twitter – The X Factor was a big one. I couldn't wait for the show to start and get on with my Twitter comments – that was part of the fun! I also loved being live on Twitter when a major Hollywood event was happening, such as the Oscars or the Golden Globes, where I would comment on celebrities who were wearing our products, and makeup and outfit looks. There was a sense of community on Twitter and there were certain people whom I didn't know in real life but felt I knew them really well. It was as if we were all on a giant sofa watching shows and gossiping.

I would always post my tweets in real time, whatever thought I had at that moment. I never planned or scripted or scheduled tweets on my personal account. It was all real and happening right now, and that made my account really exciting. I tried different tweets to test engagement. Would a tweet about a new product launch get more engagement than a tweet about an event I was attending? Some of the more typical tweets about a product just hitting the stores weren't getting as much attention as some of the more personal tweets of the type 'I just met with x to discuss our collaboration over cappuccinos.' My tweeting strategy was that there was no strategy. I would post whenever I felt like it and wouldn't force a tweet if I didn't feel like it. As a result, my tweets appeared spontaneous and more direct. I would even share with my followers my New Year's resolutions, a new fitness regime and my progress with a new diet. And they loved it! @MrsRodial became everyone's friend, everyone loved the fly-on-the-wall approach to my life behind the scenes and I loved being able to entertain, inspire and motivate my followers. Managing my Twitter handle became a whole other job on top of my day job. It would be the first thing I would think about when I woke up and the last thing I checked before I went to bed. It was full on but I had so much fun with it!

The idea of a beauty brand having a personality on social media was unique and I was the first person to run with it. It helped make the relationship with our customers even closer and more personal. It is a platform from which I can speak more candidly about my likes and dislikes, my thoughts and ideas about new products, and our followers are less inclined to be cynical or sceptical. Why? Because it's a person and not a brand talking to them. My tweets about the brand are mixed with comments about nearly missing a flight or going to the gym or obsessing over a new shoe. Or whatever happens to me in my day-to-day life regardless of whether it is related or not to the brand. It is a closeness that could not exist between a brand and its customers before, and it's exciting. It's also very authentic as I don't really have an agenda with my personal account. I just document my everyday life and I can channel my creativity while entertaining and inspiring our customers.

It's also a bit scary to think that everything I post can be read and quoted by anyone out there. I posted a tweet when we had Kylie Jenner over in London and we spent 24 hours together, and one publication took one of my tweets as the official statement of the brand on working with Kylie! I was happy with the statement, thankfully, but that made me think, you never know who is reading your tweets.

With time, I was getting a lot more confident with Twitter and so was my team. The material was endless. From behind the scenes at the office with a new sample arriving of an exciting new colour of lipstick to being about to sign a celebrity as the face of the brand, to covering behind the scenes of photoshoots and events. We didn't always need a picture although at times there was such amazing material, we would have to share it.

In a few months my followers increased from a few hundred to tens of thousands and it looked like my time on Twitter paid off. I was getting asked to do Twitter takeovers for Harvey Nichols, *Stylist* magazine and a lot of international publications, and I was really enjoying it. I was asked to give talks about social media and people started requesting my advice. I was excited that I was doing something I really enjoyed, allowing me to be creative while connecting with our customers in a very direct way.

A couple of years into Twitter, I started reading about Instagram. A lot of my friends in the fashion industry were already on Instagram and were checking it out for fashion news and inspiration. My first reaction to that was 'Twitter has already taken on my life, I don't have time to manage another platform.'

You need to be in there, my friends said, this is where all the fashion and cool people are. I had a look at it to check out how it worked. I loved the fact that there were pictures, but it would involve a big commitment of my time to put a beautiful gallery together. I signed up (still using the @MrsRodial handle, which was my signature by then).

I am never one to do something half-heartedly: I go big or I go home. Once I decided to use Instagram, I would be full on with it, posting beautiful pictures and engaging with the audience. I already had an impressive following on Twitter so it was a matter of moving some of those followers over to Instagram.

A photo shoot with *InStyle* gave me material for some behind-the-scenes pictures. These kind of shots are always fun and popular on Instagram. And I was able to follow up with the pictures from the actual shoot, which was great as it completed the perfect mini Instagram story. It wasn't just a random lovely picture … here was a pictorial storyboard of my day, the perfect way to use Instagram and engage with your followers. The pictures linked together to form a beginning, a middle and an end, and it didn't hurt that in the final shots I had my hair and make-up done and so actually looked quite good!

A holiday later in the summer gave me a lot of Instagram material. Beautiful backgrounds, sea shots, group shots of summer clothes and shoes, and the occasional picture of Rodial products against the sand. Easy peasy.

Over time, I added shots of beautiful everyday objects, such as a magazine I was reading. Coffee shots with a pair of sunglasses do very well too. I like to occasionally post a Rodial product but I would always try and give it an interesting angle or ensure that I have a story to share about this product. My gallery would never be a Rodial skincare catalogue.

When I started, I was taking all the pictures on my iPhone, and you can tell. As I got more into Instagram, I started to carry a Cyber-Shot Sony lens with me everywhere and would take pictures at every opportunity. I am at a stage right now where I won't post a picture unless it is aesthetically pleasing. Having been in love with and worked for fashion magazines since I was a girl, I naturally want to curate a beautiful feed that is on the level of a magazine editorial shoot. If you have a good eye for photography and you can get to grips with the new digital cameras and filters, there is a lot you can do as an amateur photographer.

By September 2014 I had developed a more concise Instagram strategy: posting twice a day, morning and evening. This allows me to connect with different time zones and have enough material to keep me going. If I travel or have an event or a shoot that would give me more material, I would post up to four times a day but never more as I don't want to annoy my followers.

So, Instagram worked for me. Recently, Instagram launched a new platform called Instagram's Stories that I'm really excited about! I have already grown my audience and can add short videos and pictures to share behind the scenes. But there are only so many hours in the day and I'm not sure I have quite enough time to properly curate another platform ...

What about all the other platforms out there? I have tried getting into Pinterest, read a book, set up an account. I didn't get it so gave up on that. I got really excited with Snapchat too and started an account and started posting daily everyday elements of my life. A couple of weeks into it, I stopped. Why? I spend so much time preparing and curating everything that goes on my social media right now that I cannot justify spending any time on a platform that makes its content disappear within 24 hours. I have also decided that I need to focus on just one platform and do the best I can with it as I also have a full-time job (running Rodial and NIP+FAB, remember?). I have to admit that I am still not 100 per cent convinced about Snapchat and whether it is a platform that's here to stay and can become a useful tool for the creative industries or it's just a way for teens to exchange nude selfies. We shall see.

Overnight Success Secret #10

How to Build Your Personal Brand through Social Media

1. Pick one to two platforms to focus on and do them well. You can't realistically be on more than a couple (as you do actually have a day job).
2. With social media you get back what you give so try to spend 15 minutes every day responding to comments, liking and communicating with your audience.
3. Define the subject you want to focus on and stick to it. If you are doing high fashion, stick to high fashion. If you are in the food business, post food pictures. You are developing an audience that is looking for information, inspiration, ideas. Stick to who you are and what you represent. Your audience doesn't like surprises.
4. Decide whether to have just one account for your brand or one for your brand and one for yourself. If you have the time and the resources, I advise having both.
5. Think of your social media from your audience's point of view. Social media is not a catalogue to constantly promote your products. Give something for free, motivate, inspire, give free advice and occasionally promote your products.
6. As a business and a brand, quality photography is key. Whether you take your own pictures or

hire a photographer to batch shoot, keep the style consistent.

7. Post a few times a day but don't spam your followers with tons of posts every day. I find that two to four posts per day on Instagram are the ideal number.

8. Time your posts at peak times and at times that work for you. I like to post first thing in the morning as a lot of people check their Instagram before they go to work or during their commute. I may post during lunchtime as this is another peak time and 6–8pm after work.

9. Hashtags help get your name out there and get more people to discover you. Use appropriate industry and brand hashtags and don't overdo it; a handful of hashtags are enough without looking like a spammer.

10. Enjoy the process! Social media is called social media for a reason: be social, be creative and enjoy. I believe the business owner should handle or at least give the direction of how you want your brand portrayed. Once you have found your way, you can always get your team to support but always keep an eye on the account so it's on brand.

How to Take Good Instagram Photos:

1. Use your phone to take the picture first. Don't go via the Instagram app. You can always edit and filter the image afterwards. Your phone camera will

have higher spec and will provide an overall better-quality image for you to edit at a later date.

2. Find inspiration. Browse popular pages on Instagram to see what others are posting. Follow people on Pinterest and Tumblr to find pictures to inspire you – screenshot them so that you can look back and recreate them. You can look at trending hashtags and see what beautiful images are being shared.

3. Take photos of things that inspire you and things that showcase your personality/are of interest to you, so your pictures are a representation of you as a person.

4. Good lighting! Lighting makes a huge difference to pictures. Natural lighting is the best. If you don't have natural light, play around with your filters and saturation to try and replicate this.

5. Changing up the location of your photos is a great way to keep your followers engaged and interested. Even something as simple as outdoor backgrounds can work well to help set the scene of your photo.

6. Try to keep a theme so that all pictures look great together. This is really popular at the moment. Either use the same filter for every picture or have the same colour scheme to make sure your page looks visually consistent.

7. If you like to share selfies on your Instagram account but are not quite sure on the best poses to use, there are guides on Pinterest to show what angles will work best for you. In general, taking a selfie from slightly above is flattering. You can also try

looking anywhere but directly in the camera for the effortless selfie look – 'looking over the shoulder' shots always work well.

8. Keep the image simple – offer the viewer one clear focal point. Don't clutter it with too much going on. Sometimes simpler is better!

9. Use filters and apps to help enhance your images. The ones that you see on your favourite Instagrammers' feeds are rarely the original. Great apps include: VSCO Cam, which is really popular and is free of charge to download; FaceTune, which is great for editing selfies to remove any imperfections; Whitagram is for a white background – great for those all-white minimalist clean shots.

10. Flat lays are on trend at the moment – take pictures from above. But don't just automatically put the subject in the middle, which can create a listless image with no sense of energy or direction. Sometimes going slightly off centre creates a better-looking image, unless the scene is 100 per cent symmetrical.

11

Time for a
Designer
Collaboration

All my life I have been passionate not just about beauty … fashion and design have played a big part in my life too. Beauty and fashion are very much connected – makeup and fashion trends lead each other in new directions every season. I get very excited by new trends on the catwalk and I absorb influences from what can be the subtlest elements of design. So, my love of fashion ensures that our makeup range is very much part of the fashion world; our makeup palette tunes in to the colour trends on catwalk and vice versa.

The first time I brought fashion into the brand was a collaboration with Mary Katrantzou. I had admired Mary's work for years and owned a few pieces from her collections. Mary is really talented, a graduate of Central Saint Martins College, and created a fashion sensation with her original prints featuring anything from oversized pencils to Greek monuments in striking colour combinations. Mary was on her way up, with all the top editors attending her shows and celebrities wearing her dresses. Anna Wintour was making a point of coming to London Fashion Week to see her shows, and you know when Anna Wintour is attending a show the designer really matters. Cara Delevingne, Sarah Jessica Parker and Jennifer Lawrence were wearing her dresses. This girl was hot!

I asked my PA to connect with her, say that I am a big fan and tell her that I would love to set up a meeting. We agreed to meet at the Colbert café in Sloane Square as it was close to Mary's home and our offices. Mary likes to meet later in the morning as she works until the early hours and then wakes up slightly later, very different to me, but we bonded over scrambled eggs and cappuccinos and talked about fashion and beauty for hours. It's always a great sign when you hit it off with someone in business. Who doesn't want to work with talented people that you also like?

The discussion led to the shared desire to design something together one day. I gave her some Rodial products to try and she asked me to go to her studio where she would design something for me! Since then, she has been inviting me to her shows with front-row tickets and we get to connect even more! I wore one of her dresses at our Rodial Beautiful Awards and she joined our awards committee.

During one of our coffee meetings, she told me she was looking for a sponsor for a unique show with flowers flown over from Amsterdam. She would have live music on stage and the whole show would be the most extravagant ever to go with her designs. The idea sounded very interesting. We had never sponsored a designer before (there was no excess cash for that …) but at that point we had started doing really well. I could see that it would be a great way to raise the brand awareness with the fashion press. There would be a lot of international press as well as store buyers, and being part of the show would give us exposure not only in the US but internationally as well. Our marketing teams worked together for a few months to ensure that Rodial was included in all the marketing and press material, and we did the goodie bags, filled with Rodial products, for the front rows.

It was exciting to be part of this amazing show, sitting in the front row and looking at the gorgeous models running through a corridor of flowers, almost dancing to the music and wearing the most amazing outfits. I loved every single one of them, but the final one took my breath away. Designers always leave the masterpiece until the end, and Mary certainly did that in my opinion. For the final look the model wore a beautiful beaded strapless dress with bright purple colours. It must have weighed more than I do but it was definitely a must-have piece. I made a mental note to request it for my next big event. Sadly, I didn't get it. In the world of fashion, news travels fast and someone else's PR had first dibs ... it went from the red carpet of the Golden Globes on to the Oscars, and never made it back to London. Sob!

Despite my disappointment over the dress, the sponsorship was a great investment for my business. We got a lot of press from fashion journalists who came across our products and talked about them on their social media or featured them as London Fashion Week must-haves. We even got press in Hong Kong, Russia and Germany. People who didn't know about the brand were suddenly paying attention to Rodial, referring to our presence at the Mary Katrantzou show. You never know with these things if you will get anything out of it, so I was very happy and relieved that we got a return on our investment.

Mary was also happy with the sponsorship. There is nothing better than finding a brand you actually like to complement yours, one whose products fit, which creates a synergy between the brands. At times, designers need to accept less than complementary sponsors just to cover their expenses, and the brands are not always luxury or high end or even from a relevant industry.

Next time we met, again at the Colbert (it has become our regular haunt), we were both so happy with our first experience working together that we were ready to do something more. A skincare product wouldn't make sense: it would need to be more of a lifestyle product. At the time I was designing a limited edition candle for the holidays and my team had put together some ideas for the encasement that I wasn't happy with – Bingo! What if Mary could design the candle and also work with me on the fragrance? Mary loved the idea and we started working immediately. Straight away, she began sending me ideas for the printed glass and I started sending her fragrance options. Within three months we had the fragrance and design secured; a beautiful candle that featured printed crystals of pink and lavender that looked three-dimensional!

The candle launched in autumn 2011 with all our retailers, from Harvey Nichols to Harrods and Space NK, and in all our 35 countries. Everyone wanted a piece of the Rodial/Mary Katrantzou collaboration! In some department stores they would put the candle in the fashion departments too, next to Mary's collection. We garnered huge social media coverage as the candle photographed so well. Our customers were becoming very creative with the uses of it and, after burning it, they would use the printed casing as a makeup brush glass or to store pencils or hair bands. It was a beautiful thing and I love seeing it as a part of people's lives.

Our collaboration also became a PR success. Mary and I hosted a tea party at the penthouse of the Soho Hotel and all magazines attended and covered, from *Vogue* to *InStyle* to *Grazia*. We also got the international press interested and the candle was covered by the likes of *Elle*, *Allure* and *Bazaar* in the US and Germany. The collaboration took a lot of work, it was a steep learning curve for me and my team, but it was a massive success and I knew I would do more of these in the future.

When we launched our new makeup in the autumn of 2014, fronted by Daisy Lowe, I wanted a designer item as part of the collection. I am always looking outside beauty and into fashion and art for inspiration, and I wanted to keep up with the direction of collaborating with a designer. I met with my team and explained the situation and we brainstormed over pizza and wine. And the idea just popped up! Instead of going to an established designer, why don't we go to the source of talent and get an up-and-coming designer from a design college? The ultimate college for design talent is London's Central Saint Martins College, from where some of the most successful designers have graduated. I knew about it over the years from books and articles featuring its superstar graduates, including Alexander McQueen, John Galliano and Stella McCartney.

What if I got to brief the students to create an object for us? I could show them how to design with a brand in mind, and brief them about the target market, the practical considerations and the commercial aspects of a project, and then manufacture this object and sell it in our stores. What an amazing experience and opportunity this would be for a student. As we had decided not to do another awards show, this could be something new, something equally good for the brand but also something where we could give something back. And so the Rodial Art & Design Challenge was born ... an initiative that is true to my heart and all about investing in education and young talent.

My team connected with the Central Saint Martins people and they were very keen. A month later, in January 2015, I was at the college briefing the second-year BA students on a competition to develop a design for a Rodial makeup-brush case.

The students were from all over the world – I think I counted 15 different nationalities among the 25 students ... I felt great meeting those students as I love to nurture new talent. At work, I am surrounded by a young, dynamic team and I am interviewing constantly to ensure I keep this energy coming into the business. Young, new talent is important for innovation, breaking the rules and revolutionising our industry. I would treat the students as part of my team and I would work with them every step of the way. I took them through our entire development process, showing them how a project went from a concept, through design and production, to being on the shop floor and in the handbags of Rodial customers around the world. I remember the excitement I felt at seeing my initial product for the first time and getting my first magazine features: it was infectious, the more exposure I got, the more I wanted. It was the greatest buzz to see something you have created selling out at Harrods or being tweeted about by Ellie Goulding, and I wanted this to be an incentive for the students too.

I met the students three more times, listening to everyone's presentations, giving feedback and seeing them really progress and improve their designs. The process of deciding on the winner wasn't easy. I decided to offer something more to the students and bring a few more expert judges on board from different areas and get them to give their point of view.

The first person I thought of was my friend Henry Holland, the fashion designer. Henry gained attention with his bold, 1980s-inspired T-shirts that displayed catchphrases such as 'I'll tell you who's boss, Kate Moss' in the 2000s, and he founded his own fashion house, House of Holland. He has also become an established TV personality, co-hosting shows alongside Alexa Chung and working as a judge on a number of TV shows. I met Henry years ago and really loved his aesthetic; he had created a variety of different accessories from phone cases to nails and he had an eye for combining fashion and trends with an everyday item. His advice would be invaluable.

My next judge was supermodel Erin O'Connor. Erin has been on multiple covers of fashion magazines including Italian *Vogue* and has regularly appeared on catwalk shows in Milan and Paris modelling for top houses such as Chanel, Gucci and Fendi. She also modelled in print ads for top designers like John Galliano, Christian Dior, Jean-Paul Gaultier, Donna Karan, Prada, Versace, Miu Miu and others. She has appeared on several high-profile television shows over the years and she would be my perfect partner-in-crime on this project.

Daniela Rinaldi joined me from Harvey Nichols. I had known Daniela for years as she was always a supporter of the brand, and her involvement would ensure that the product would be commercially viable. I wanted to get her excited and get the product into Harvey Nichols with a lot of buzz and, of course, her stamp of approval.

I also invited Jackie Annesley, Editor of Style for the *Sunday Times*, to join us and provide a press point of view – we needed to ensure that the design we picked would appeal to the press and the 'Style' section of the *Sunday Times* is a trend-setting publication, always first to report new trends and take risks.

I invited our entire panel to join me at Central Saint Martins to meet the five finalists. First arrived Erin looking very cool and natural in white leather jacket and jeans. She had all the student presentations sent to her the previous week and she came in very much prepared with notes and questions to ask. Erin is a very warm person and took her role as judge of this challenge very seriously! Henry arrived next, very upbeat as always and ready to start. He is always frank and sharp with his comments, and I couldn't wait to see what he had to say. Daniela is very warm and friendly and I knew she would be very supportive of the students and their designs. Finally, Jackie arrived – I had heard that she is very good at expressing her opinions and I was looking forward to her very different point of view.

So myself and my four fellow judges sat behind a large table, next to each other, ready to meet the students. Every single one of the finalists presented us with their research, inspiration, prototype and a short film they had prepared to share their journey of designing the Rodial makeup-brush case.

All five designs were so different. Some were very design led while not being that practical and others were more practical with a simpler design. I had seen the cases before but the judges were viewing them for the first time and started testing them. One of the cases looked like a Céline evening bag with open sides but when Erin put the brushes in, closed it and moved it from side to side the brushes fell out. Another was so heavy that Jackie feared for the customer's foot if, God forbid, they dropped it in the bathroom. Another one was too plain and Henry thought it would be better suited as a free gift with a purchase. I was getting really worried that we wouldn't be able to pick a winner.

Slowly all the judges started leaning towards a black case which had lots of zips that you could use to hold individual brushes. It seemed modern and unique, and the zips made it look fresh. Interestingly, this was the case that had always stood out to me. The designer behind this case was a Hong Kong student called Aaron Chung. At our first session he had presented a hard wooden case, which wasn't on brand or on brief at all, and I asked him to change the design. He spoke to his course leader and almost quit. His tutor convinced him to stay and so he changed the design based on my feedback. Here he was now, having made it through six months' of work and selection processes to be in the top five and very close to winning.

I thanked the students and took some pictures with them and the panel. When the students left, I deliberated with my fellow judges. Everyone loved Aaron's case. We had a clear winner!

I didn't want it to announce it there and then in front of all the students. I decided to ask their course leader to tell them in private about the results rather than having to face the disappointment of four students live. They were all winners in my mind as they had all improved their presentation skills and all evolved as designers. I enjoyed working with them and I hope they enjoyed the project too!

To announce the winner formally, the panel and I hosted a VIP dinner at the Balthazar restaurant in Covent Garden. I picked a private space in the restaurant as I wanted to create a very intimate atmosphere with the judges, all our friends and the five finalists. It was all about the students and it was important to get them involved, introduce them to our guests and keep it informal.

To wrap up the project I commissioned a photoshoot of Erin and me with the Rodial makeup brushes from renowned photographer Greg Williams. Over the years, I had heard of Greg's work and always wanted to work with him. He had done shoots for Victoria Beckham, Sienna Miller, Brad Pitt, Rosie Huntington-Whiteley and Robert Downey Jr. I wanted to do a fun shoot with the brushes that would go into the makeup case. Greg directed us to perfection and the pictures looked amazing. We ended up not only with some beautiful pictures but also a lot of content for YouTube and social media.

This project with the students was very close to my heart and one of the happiest moments in my career. Since then I have been trying to allocate some time every year to mentor students and up-and-coming entrepreneurs. This also led me to an opportunity to be a guest mentor on a US TV show, *Project Runway Fashion Startup*, where I mentored a young jewellery entrepreneur, who would be pitching her business to secure financing from four investors including designer Rebecca Minkoff. Tommy Hilfiger was also a key mentor on the show and it was such an honour for me to be included. Mentoring on camera was a brand new experience for me but, hey, I am all about taking risks, so I was happy to have ticked that box!

Overnight Success Secret #11

Collaborations 101

One of the best and least expensive ways to grow your audience is by collaborating with other brands. Look out for opportunities to collaborate with other like-minded brands in complementary industries to yours. With no money being exchanged, you offer them access to your audience and they will give you access to theirs.

These are my top ten tips for a collaboration:

1. Identify brands that are at a similar level to yours. For example, if you are just starting out find brands that are just starting out as well. You need to be realistic and ask yourself, what can I offer this brand and what can I get in return? If you have very little to give and a lot to gain, then you won't be taken seriously. By contrast, if you find a brand with a similar size audience or social media following, then you both should gain from the partnership.

2. Go for a brand that is excited about what you do, your products or services, and will be very enthusiastic about this collaboration. Successful collaborations need the commitment and enthusiasm of all parties.

3. Don't doubt yourself: we all have something to offer. If you find it hard to articulate your strengths and what you can offer to another brand, ask a friend to help you. Sometimes we are hard on ourselves and we need someone else to tell us what we are good at.

4. Do your research. There is so much information on social media and online that you can narrow down the brands that you are interested in.

5. Collaborations can take different forms, from a digital campaign to a co-branded product. When you are just starting out, try a digital or a social media collaboration with another brand to test the waters. You can find out if the fit is good and if their audience is relevant to your brand. Once you test the waters and you see that a partnership would work, you can move to the next level of a co-branded product.

6. Define clearly the parameters of a partnership. Don't always assume that the other party will have the same ideas in mind. Clearly define the scope, deliverables and what each party is responsible for and agree in writing before taking the first step.

7. Be creative with the industries you look at: for me, beauty and fashion are always an easy match but you can look at a less obvious connection to a brand with a similar audience to yours. Just do your research.

8. When the partnership goes ahead, make sure you shout about it and you promote it on all your platforms (of course, this needs to be reciprocated by the other brand): social media accounts, newsletters, homepage on the website, blog. And don't do a one-off job – you need to be creating anticipation and stretching the news over a period of time.

9. If a collaboration goes well, think of how you can take it to the next level. If something works, improve and repeat.

10. Focus on a handful of brands and go deeper. Doing too many collaborations and jumping from one collaboration to another can be dangerous. While you may gain a new audience, you don't want to alienate your existing one.

12

Build Your Personal Brand

As this book is about achieving business success, then I can't really avoid talking about 'The Brand'. You will have heard the word tossed around in magazines, in interviews, on TV, and in these pages ... in fact, it is difficult to avoid. I am sure you know what it means, or at least you think you do. That's the thing about the word 'brand': it is a little bit slippery. It can mean many things and one thing ... sorry, now I am being slippery. The point is you need to know what it means for your business and for you. And what is the process of creating a brand.

All brands go through a process of development until they become superbrands. One famous example is Coca-Cola. In the early days, Coke was just one of many sodas on the shelf, but the company decided to try and stand out from the other bottles. They went on to dominate the market, so much so that even now you find yourself asking for a Coke when what you really mean is a cola.

Why did they dominate ... it can't just be the shape of the bottle, can it? Well, no. They and many others like them expanded the word 'brand' into something much bigger, much broader. It was a feeling, it was an emotion, it was a world ... and a world you wanted to be part of. In a market of similar products all with similar price-points competing for business, the battle was on for consumer loyalty and share – how do we get them to buy ours instead of theirs? Simply shouting your name loudest or advertising generic features didn't work. What they needed was a bit of 'extra edge'.

The most successful brands are aspirational. We are after a Chanel bag or a Saint Laurent leather jacket or a pair of Louboutin boots because we want a piece of the lifestyle that the brand can bestow upon us ... a little reflected sunlight. We want to be in that gang, be one of the sort of people who know the difference, who are connected enough to know where to get those exclusive heels, who can appreciate the quality of that bag, we can't help it. We are all a little bit tribal. There are similar bags, leather jackets and stilettos but the reason we desire more products from these brands is because we don't buy a product, we buy a lifestyle. 'Lifestyle' suggests a choice. You are not stuck with the life your parents had or the life that you have now … you can literally 'style your life'. It goes against the old Freudian theory that you are somehow 'programmed' in your first five years and instead suggests that you are the sum of your passions, knowledge, eccentricities and experiences. You can change who you are, you can reinvent yourself, you can create your own image.

As much as it is important to define the brand that is your business, it is equally or even more important to develop your own personal brand. Why? You can give the brand personality and get your audience to relate with you on a personal level, which makes it easier to buy your product or service or whatever you are out there to promote. Getting eyeballs on your brand isn't enough … people want to feel they are sharing the experience with you.

Your aspirations might be to become a successful entrepreneur and build a successful business, not to become a celebrity. Being an entrepreneur must surely be a waste of time for the vain, the ones who get into a business in order to boost their profile. Well, not quite. The reality is that as a brand owner you represent your brand and, if you want your brand to be recognised, you need to build your personal brand too. Your company and your personal brand go hand in hand.

Of course, there are examples of people who have successful businesses and have remained anonymous, and no one knows their name. But with the culture that we live in these days, it becomes more and more difficult to have a successful business if you are hidden in anonymity. And we are not talking about pop-star famous. You just need to become an expert in your field, to be recognised, to be quoted and to be respected. It used to be that the only people who had a personal brand were celebrities. Now, with social media, anyone can build and amplify their brand image and become a celebrity in their own field. Social media has changed the way a brand or a personality is built by providing a platform where you can shape the world's perception of you. Social media has revolutionised the way brands and people communicate with their audiences and amplify messages, so it is even more important to carefully build the brand that is you.

When you are an entrepreneur, you are your brand. What is a brand? A brand is your identity and how people perceive you. Creating your own brand is an art. Your personal branding aligns what you want people to think about you with what they actually think about you. So how do you start shaping your own personal brand? What is your story, what are you good at, what are your marketable qualities? Write all this down. Then think of how you want people to perceive you. What do you want them to think after they have met you? Does your current situation match what you want to be known for? If not, then you need to put together a plan of action to develop your personal brand and get it to where you want it to be.

So, brands are not just consumer products or corporations any more: they are you and me. Look at the Kardashian brand. The Kardashian brand has been developing over the last ten years consistently with a plan and a lot of decision-making along the way. Love or hate them, the Kardashians have developed a very strong personal brand. This brand took a while to build. When they first started with season 1 of their reality TV show, *Keeping up with the Kardashians*, very few people knew about the family. They were an average American family that were trying to make a name for themselves. Fast forward ten years and the Kardashian brand is very well defined, starting with the way they look: sleek hair and makeup, body-conscious clothing, showcasing their assets. They are icons to girls, women and, yes, men all over the world. They are the antithesis of the skinny models as they are women with curves who feel equally at ease in a bejewelled Balmain gown and a pair of Topshop ripped jeans.

Kim's brand evolved over the years and became more sophisticated – from doing shoots with B-list magazines to making it to the cover of the US *Vogue* and *Bazaar* and rubbing shoulders with the most iconic people in fashion such as Karl Lagerfeld, Carine Roitfeld and Anna Wintour. To understand the Kardashians' journey, all you need to do is watch the first episode of season one of the series and you'll understand the progress. It is a fascinating story of how the world of media, both social and old school, works today ... and how it is rapidly evolving. If the Kardashians had come out ten years earlier things might have been very different, but they hit a moment when TV shows could be fed by the recently emerging social media and the explosion of gossip magazines: this cross-pollination was something new. In fact, the viewing figures for the TV show have been steadily falling ... but it doesn't matter, they have a much more consistent and instant platform for their brand through online and social media engagement.

Maintaining the Kim Kardashian brand is not easy. First of all, it takes a lot of maintenance. Kim won't ever leave the house without hair, makeup and styling. When you are such a well-defined brand, you can't be seen going to the grocery store wearing old sweats and sneakers. Although if she did – and nothing is off limits in the Krazy world of the Kardashians – the sweats would be designer, with brand new sneakers, full hair and makeup and oversize sunglasses: it probably takes three hours to create that casual look ... You get the point.

When she travels for fashion weeks or other events, there is always a glam team around, whether they travel together, which is usually the case, or she engages local teams (many celebs will have a team of trusted freelancers in Europe, a New York team, an LA team, a Paris team and so on, depending on where they are in the world). Outfits are planned for every step of the trip, from the airport outfits to the day-after outfits to the big events and appearances. Outfits take a team of stylists a week of work plus endless alterations to ensure the fit is perfect. The clothes are also very well defined. Always body conscious, a little transparency and cleavage here and there. The Kardashians are not following fashion trends but are aware of them and they are incorporated in their own style. And this makes them relatable to their audience.

And then there is the beauty grooming: endless spray tans, workout sessions, beauty treatments and cosmetic enhancements. You can never relax. Perfection takes time, and it's ongoing. Kim makes it all look effortless, though. Hair and makeup sessions at 4am to get ready for filming? Tick. Back-to-back spray tans at midnight to be ready for the next day's shoot? Tick. Regular sessions at the dermatologist? Tick. It takes effort, commitment and investment to look like Kim Kardashian. And that is the brand she is selling.

None of this is new territory for celebrities. This is the same regime Hollywood stars have been following for years. Studios such as MGM had celebrity fixers who would not only ensure the stars wore the right gown and had the latest hair do, they would fix them up with other stars to maximise their appeal, or promote a new movie. The publicity machine was rigorously controlled. Stories would be invented, stories would be supressed: the important thing was that the studio image and the star's 'brand' were getting the right sort of exposure. Then the movie business changed. Actors were no longer the 'property' of the studios and they could do what they liked ... and often did. They were seen falling out of limos, they were caught in compromising positions with underworld spies or the wife of a close friend, and yes, they were papped in old sweats going to the grocery store, and the illusion was shattered. Sunset Boulevard suddenly looked like a real-life documentary ... the man behind the curtain was exposed. 'The end of an era,' they cried.

But for all the nostalgic tears and 'they don't make 'em like they used to' complaints about the new style of film star, things were not all bad. Suddenly the stars were 'real' and approachable. They lived in the same world as we did ... the dreams we had of one day bumping into them were no longer dreams, they could conceivably come true. These rare creatures didn't cease to exist when not on the silver screen, they were here among us ... apparently doing grocery shopping. Some kept their private lives private and managed themselves as though they were in a mini studio system – they controlled the times they would allow pictures and punch photographers the rest of the time. Others embraced the role of celebrity and made every moment of their lives an opportunity to be seen and loved by the fans … known in showbiz as being 'always on'.

The Kardashians and their ilk have taken this 'always on' ideal and reinvented it for the modern age, and it is a million times more intense than it ever was. Movie magazines and gossip columns came out weekly: the Kardashians are being discussed and seen seemingly every minute of the day.

But that's not the only way to make yourself into a brand. There is another kind of modern brand phenomenon where the person has travelled a different path. One person has achieved such a transformation and created such a strong brand for themselves that they can sell anything under that brand … that person is Victoria Beckham.

Going from a Spice Girl to an internationally recognised style icon and fashion designer launching her own range in 2008 – that's no easy feat and it didn't happen overnight. Before launching her own range, she had been collaborating with other brands and fashion designers, getting her name out there with the right associations to establish herself as a player in the fashion world. She changed her style, moving from tight, short and colourful dresses and platform heels to the work of more sophisticated and fashion-forward designers, changing hair and makeup looks to reflect the new style. Every one of her appearances is carefully planned. Whether arriving at an airport, leaving a hotel to go to a meeting or on a family outing, her hair and makeup are always flawless, the oversize black sunglasses are always there and she has a well-planned look (usually from her upcoming collection). And it is not just about having the money to invest in this. It takes a lot of discipline and determination to keep up the image of your brand 24/7.

Another example of someone in control of her brand is Gigi Hadid. Gigi has evolved from being just a model to becoming a personality. There are thousands of models out there but Gigi is an example of a model who stands out from all the rest. She is pretty but there are equally pretty models out there. She is 22 and has a natural beauty. She could behave as any other normal 22-year-old and throw on an old pair of jeans and a T-shirt when she's not on a photo shoot or the catwalk, but all her looks are carefully planned and managed. When she is doing the shows in NY or Paris, she has a whole set of outfits planned for her. Arrival at the airport, leaving the hotel, going to the show, at the after-party ... each is an opportunity for maximum online exposure and each involves a carefully styled version of herself. She is not leaving hair and makeup to chance either. Unlike a lot of models, she works with specific hair and makeup artists for her non-show looks so that she can keep her look and brand consistent. She regularly works with Kardashian stylist Monica Rose to ensure she always looks on trend and, in fact, often she will create the trends.

A lot of this has to do with her innate style, of course. Yes, she works with stylists, but contrary to popular belief most good stylists don't work with clients who have no idea. They work with people who already have a strong look and they are there to do the leg work. They act as an advisor, they look at the 'brand' of the client and work to that brief, putting the looks together and even packing up looks to send on to the next destination and the next photo call.

Gigi is a smart girl and knows that to be a fashion icon you need to work on it and be very disciplined, and she does an amazing job at it. She has developed her own personal identity on and off duty. We all love seeing her in gowns and designer clothes at the shows but what she is most known for are her off-duty looks: ripped or leather jeans, crop tops and long coats. Together with Zayn Malik, she has become a style icon and is always one step ahead of a lot of other more forgettable models. She is the one everyone is looking out for ... she is top of the online model searches to see what her latest after-show outfit is, what she wears when working out or heading out on the town. She's become such a personality brand that she is now not only getting endorsement deals as a model but also collaboration opportunities ... such as her latest collaboration with Tommy Hilfiger, where she helped design the TommyxGigi range for their more affordable 'Tommy' brand. She not only designed the range but also modelled for it and hosted the party. This is the power of a person who as a brand stands out from the competition and has elevated herself to the next level of recognition and celebrity.

This is why the brands Kardashian, Beckham and Gigi, even though they are extremely different to each other, have a lot in common: carefully planned images, consistency and keeping it up for years. Evolution plays a big part in any brand, as well: you can't keep on doing the same things. You need to evolve and offer your audience something new and interesting while keeping up the principles of your brand.

Yeah, yeah, you might say, but I am not a supermodel, I haven't got a mad family and I wasn't around for Girl Power ... what does this mean to me and what can I learn from these stories? How can I implement these examples to develop my own brand?

Well, first of all I agree that you are probably not a supermodel, curvaceous reality star or pouty design phenomenon. You are you. And you are the only you out there. You are utterly unique – your style, your personality, your insight are 100 per cent original. No matter what your brand actually is and does, be it selling beauty products, fashion tips or piston engines, it starts with you. You are the face of the brand ... and if you are starting out small, that's often all you have. So use it.

When you look at a celeb Instagram feed, at first glance it looks nothing more than pics of the celebrity in various locations, reposted pap shots, one or two plates of food, random body parts and the odd mirror selfie. But look closer and you will see that the hashtags to these shots are often naming or recommending a product. Here I am trying #brandname makeup, or great night at the #brandname club and so on. You are following the story of their day-to-day life but you are also being sold something ... and you don't mind, because it feels good to be part of the community. Sharing feels good. Well, you can be the celebrity of your own brand. You can use the same techniques. Here are some ways to get the most out of your online brand.

Tell Your Story

I am going to assume you know what your brand/product/thing is. Now you have to get it out there. Before you stumble online blurting out whatever comes into your head, think about your vision for the brand. Just as Gigi plans her looks, you need to plan your online assault. Think of it as telling the story of your brand. Stories are the most basic form of communication. No matter how sophisticated we get, humans will always need stories. So, tell us yours. If your brand is just starting out then involve us in the development. Kickstarter does this really well, encouraging each of the Kickstarters to send their backers regular updates on progress up to and beyond the funding deadline. It fosters a real sense of community among the backers and crucially between the customer and the producer. You could start with how you got here ... what made you want to start this brand ... what sent you down this road. We are with you for the launch, we are with you when the print company spells your name wrong ... and we are with you wherever the story goes. You could even go so far as to plot a little movie-style storyboard for your online campaign if it helps you focus on a direction.

Having said all of that, you should also remember that this story is going out LIVE! It's an ongoing, organic story and anything can, and probably will, happen. So be flexible and, where appropriate, take your followers with you. I say 'if appropriate' because there are things you may not wish to share: it's probably not a good idea to moan about money troubles or problems with the actual product. Try and keep things positive. Even though it may be true, we don't want to hear that you are starting this just because you got fired and had to do something to live. We want to hear that suddenly being free from your old job gave you the opportunity you'd been waiting for to follow your dream. Same story, different tone.

Finally, practise telling your story – have a couple of good versions of it ready for pitches, for interviews and to include in your posts. You may have heard of the 'elevator pitch'. It's a movie term for the 30 seconds you get (not necessarily in an elevator) to pitch your idea to the movie producer you have managed to corner. 'It's like *Die Hard* meets *Bambi* set in outer space' ... that kind of thing. Have an elevator pitch for your brand ready to go. It should excite, intrigue and, without telling the whole story, give enough info about what the brand is to make me excited to hear more.

You Talking to Me?

I have spoken about being yourself but you need to be yourself in company. By that I mean remember who you are talking to. Do you have an audience in mind? The pitch you might do for a teen audience would (I hope) be quite different to the one you'd give to West Hendon Ladies Conservative Club. They'd both come from you, but one might be you with your 'telephone voice' on. Think about which works best ... ideally you can just be wonderfully you and all the world will love you, but it's worth thinking about.

Know who you are selling to/targeting ... this is going to help you build your community and your fan base. Look at the other stuff your target group might be into. Who else do they follow? What else do they buy? What blogs are out there? Immerse yourself in the world you want to be a part of, and remember you don't just want one kind of flower: your community needs to include influencers, peers, friends, superfans and casual passers-by ... they will all help you to build your brand and your personality.

Collaborate and Propagate

OK, we have spoken about identifying your audience, but how can you get maximum exposure for your brand? Well, in your research you will have found things your target group is into, the things they like and the people they follow. It's time to reach out. Talk directly to some of the contacts you have made. It may be that someone is making a complementary product you can work with ... even if it's just agreeing to namecheck or recommend each other. If the product is right, you could go further. If you are selling skate decks, get one signed by a famous skater and run a comp to win it ... better still, ask them to design a deck that you will produce. It's exactly the same principle behind my collaborations with Central Saint Martins and Mary Katrantzou ... the brands complemented each other without directly competing. However you do it – and I'm sure you know best what would work for your brand – is up to you, but the more you can get your name and your product out there the better ... and if it's for free that's a double bonus!

Another way to get your brand talked about is by offering to write a piece for a small blog relevant to your sector. They are generally happy for content and as long as your brand fits in with their normal editorial content, then they'll generally be glad to have someone fill some column inches. Mention your brand but don't overdo it ... it may be that your topic is the problem your particular brand can solve. You can embed a video, do what you like, but make it relevant to the readers. If all you get is a few extra followers from the blog then that's all good, you've not lost anything. However, what you are hoping for is for it to go viral. If your story is compelling enough and your idea original enough it may just get reposted on bigger blogs, on news sites or even picked up by TV news. Free press!

The internet has a voracious appetite. How do you think the bloggers and writers find their material? They need to put something out every day so they are constantly scanning the internet for stuff to write about ... and if you have targeted your product in the right way, and got your story straight, you could go from a handful to hundreds of thousands of followers in less than a day. And it cost you nothing. You could soon be having that interview on the *BBC Breakfast* sofa ... and when you do, remember your elevator pitch!

Hello ... It's Me Again

Keep your story fresh. While I have stated that you shouldn't come across as a stalker, it can't hurt to 'reintroduce' yourself from time to time. If you are already known in the industry in which you have decided to strike out, then you may need to start by telling people who you are now. They may remember you as the girl who did graphic design PR at company X: you need to reintroduce yourself to these existing contacts in your new persona.

Beyond the contacts who already know you and need re-educating, there are those who are meeting you for the first time. Not everyone will love what you have to offer at first sight, so every now and again re-launch yourself to the world. You could base this around a new version of your product or an offshoot. When we launched Nip+Fab, it benefited Rodial as it reminded people that we were out there and brought more traffic to all of our platforms. Fashion models are constantly updating their book with new pictures, new Z-Cards and Polaroids, always putting the latest shots upfront. So you should be refreshing the way people see your brand: if they see the same old pic every time they scroll on to your Facebook page, no matter how great it might be, they will soon turn off. Take another great shot and use that.

To support the 'you are your brand' idea, regardless of what your brand name or online handle might be, it's also a good idea to have an Instagram account or website in your name. You should already have bought up as many variations of your brand name as you can on all the relevant platforms, and if you include a website in your own name it's another way people can find you and another way to keep your profile in the rankings. As well as the brand identities Rodial and Nip+Fab and posting as MrsRodial, I also maintain a site at www.mariahatzistefanis.com, which links to all the other identities.

Overnight Success Secret #12

How to Develop Your Own Brand

So how do you go from being a founder of a business to becoming a brand? Find some role models around you, people who have set up similar businesses to yours, people you admire. Study their personal brand. What is so special about them? What makes them stand out?

Keep a biography with your biggest achievements and a selection of good-quality portrait pictures you can use for press and online articles about yourself. Update this at least once a year or when you have something new to add. When you write the biography, always take a step back and think how a journalist would write this. What elements of your background and business so far would be interesting to the press? If the biography sounds exciting to you, it will sound exciting to the press; if it already bores you, start again. Your biography has to be informative and snappy, emphasising the most interesting accomplishments. Keep this on file ready to be sent out but also to remind yourself of your achievements and how far you have come with your business.

These are my top five steps to develop your own brand:

1. Think of yourself as a product, a commodity, a brand. Every time you see the YSL logo, you think high fashion, edgy, fashion forward, opulent. You need to find your own look.

2. Be true to yourself and imagine an improved version of you. Think of yourself at your best times and think of how you can develop that brand on an ongoing basis so that you are instantly recognisable.

3. Differentiate yourself from the competition. Depending on your industry and your job, there are countless people out there like you doing the same job in the same industry. By branding yourself and standing out from the competition, you become unique and memorable, and you get an elevated status and recognition from the rest. If all else is equal, if you have a strong personal brand your product will have a higher brand awareness, will be more desirable and ultimately you will beat your competition and reach your goals of success.

4. Be original. You can always be inspired by others, but unless you are original and have something new to say you won't go very far. And remember, it's just not about the look. You need to be able to tell your own story so that people pay attention and so that you can develop a long-lasting brand. Lady Gaga's choices are not always stylish or elegant but she is always original and we remember her for that. She has a very strong visual brand identity for herself.

5. Your brand needs to be strong and consistent, from the way you look to the values you represent and the way you speak. You develop a persona that best represents you and you keep it consistent. The brand identity doesn't mean that everyone will like it but they will recognise it and you'll become known for it.

13 Get on the Best-Dressed Lists

You really don't need to get on the best-dressed lists but how you look really defines your brand. You may ask yourself, how is all this celebrity branding business relevant to you? You are not in showbiz or in any other industry that requires you to look flawless for the paparazzi 24/7 and you don't have the budget for it either. However, if you are a small business, if you are just starting out or in the early years of development, YOU are the brand. You need to always put your best foot forward to make a good impression for your brand. As well as cultivating a consistent attitude and tone of voice to your online presence, it will really help to have a strong and distinctive look.

A big turning point for me in thinking about image and personal branding came from the two occasions I worked with Kylie Jenner and seeing first-hand the work that goes in to creating her brand. The first time we did a shoot together, she flew over her own hair and makeup artist. This could be criticised as grandstanding … but when you have a very specific image and you have a trusted team of people that know how to create it, you need to stick to those people, especially when you have an important photoshoot for a campaign. This is not the time to be experimenting with a new hair and makeup team. Also, when you have your own team with you, you can relax and get mentally prepared for the shoot or the interview without having to worry about how you will end up looking. Just like Gigi, Kylie had her outfits planned in advance, with different outfits for the shoot, photo call, live interview, press interviews and *InStyle* tea party that we were hosting on that day.

At one point when we were about to do the photo-call pictures, her assistant took some snaps of her on the phone. She looked at them and something wasn't right. She was wearing a black semi-sheer top with a black bra. And the bra was really showing in the pictures! Disaster! She wouldn't go to the photo call like this. Celebrities know that what looks good in everyday life and in the mirror doesn't necessarily translate to what shows in the pictures, especially when it comes to semi-sheer materials. Thank God we were at the Westfield shopping centre so we could send one of our assistants to buy a new nude bra that wouldn't show through in the pictures. The assistant came back slightly breathless but very pleased with herself, a shopping bag clutched in her hand ... mission accomplished. We quickly got the bra out and ... oh dear. It was a size 32A. Fair enough, we hadn't discussed size before she left but 32A for Kylie? Are you kidding me? Off the assistant went, red-faced, back to the store to get the appropriate size. Finally, with a nude bra in the right size, we retook some test-shots on the iPhone and everybody was happy. This delayed us by half an hour but you need to do what you need to do, and undergarments do matter!

After we finished the morning session, she went to her hotel room to have a nap and had full face and makeup done again for our afternoon sessions. Not a little powder and update the lipstick ... all the two-hour prep and the entire face re-done for the second time that day. This is the level of attention to detail and commitment that it takes to look good and keep up your image. It was an eye-opener for me. Kylie and her team left nothing to chance.

It was quite an experience to work closely with a celebrity who is so disciplined about her look. I also loved the way Kylie experimented by wearing new designers. For one of her looks she was wearing a black and white dress by British designer David Koma. I've also seen her sister Kendall and Gigi Hadid wearing his dresses in the past and got really intrigued. I looked him up and got a few pieces from his collection and really loved his style: it suited my body shape and made me feel super powerful. I went to his studio in east London and met with him, we became friends and I ended up walking the red carpet with him, wearing one of his stunning dresses at the Fashion Awards in December 2016. What a moment!

I am not suggesting that you need to travel with an army of stylists and makeup artists, but I am saying that attention to detail in how you and your posts look is vital to the success of your online brand. And it is worth noting here that backgrounds count too. It's a waste of time if you look amazing but your picture background is a pile of dirty pants on an unmade bed, but for now let's get back to you and how your look can amplify or even be your brand.

Dress for success. Don't dress for the job you have, dress for the job you want. If you analyse the looks of celebrities, they are immaculate all the time. They don't have days off. They develop an image, a look that involves the way they dress, how they do their hair and makeup. This is their distinctive style that makes them unique and different to everyone else. It's their signature and people know them for it.

Developing a look for yourself usually takes time and a lot of trial and error: it's the same for many celebrities. It is an evolutionary process and one in which potentially you have to take a few risks in developing a look that represents you and your brand.

Ideally you already have or can develop a look that is distinctive and consistent so people recognise you for it. Kate Moss has her laid-back glam rock vibe – she wears lots of low-waisted jeans, boots, floaty dresses, leopard-skin and leather. Her hair always looks undone in a 'I'm not trying too hard' way and she usually has a 'no makeup' look. Kim Kardashian, on the other hand, has a polished look with figure-hugging outfits, lots of transparency and lots of cleavage showing. Likewise, her hair and makeup will be done to perfection. Both of these iconic women have a different look and they stick to it with a few variations.

Your own look could start with a certain hair colour or hair do, sticking to a certain style of clothes or a specific colour palette. Experiment with makeup and see what works for you ... because there is only one you! You need to remember to celebrate and exploit your uniqueness. Not everyone is *Vogue*-cover material but you need to use what you have got to your advantage. Lots of freckles? Then make that your thing! Only four foot eight inches tall? Make a feature of it ... be the small chick with a big attitude. Gap in your front teeth? Get those unique incisors out there and take a big bite ... own that look. Be influenced but don't try to look the same as anyone else. Do it your way. Being unique means exactly that ... so be unique!

My personal look has evolved massively over the last few years. I need to look well put-together during the day at work and in meetings in a 'beauty entrepreneur at the office' kinda way ... but I can turn it up when I am invited to events in the evening. I wasn't always so 'en pointe' and had to learn the hard way. I admit, I had a closet full of clothes that I never wore, several outfits that I'd like to forget (but I can't, they are burned into my memory like a childhood trauma) and I had lazy days where I didn't do my hair and makeup ... obviously, these were the days that I'd bump into someone I wanted to make an impression on. I even showed up at an event once completely unprepared, looking like I'd just rolled out of bed (I had actually come straight from a rather stressful day at work) only to find a gaggle of photographers taking my picture. Horrors!

That was the moment I realised that being successful and looking good at all times go together.

How did I do it? Going through and editing my wardrobe was a top priority. This can be really hard, especially if you are a hoarder – but it's important to clear up your wardrobe and identify what looks good on you and get rid of the rest. Have the vision of your ideal self in mind at all times as you do it.

First, I had to get my basic look right. I always loved dark colours and was wearing a lot of black … that always made me feel put together. I also knew what shapes worked for me. I am happy with my legs and arms but I tend to gain all my weight on my tummy, so I avoid anything low cut or anything that accentuates the waist. I like showing a bit of leg but then everything else needs to be covered, and I'll wear a sandal or interesting shoe to show my legs off. Once I'd got rid of the lime-green hoodies, ra-ra skirts and Duran Duran 1987 tour T-shirts lurking in the dark recesses of my wardrobe, it all fell into place. I knew what looked good on me all along, really, I just needed the self-discipline to dress that way every day.

But how do you develop a look?

1. Be realistic in the way you want to look based on your body shape. Dress to enhance your assets rather than go with the trends that may not suit you.
2. Look at the trends but think: where will I wear that? Always invest in items that you can effortlessly incorporate into your daily life, rather than wait for a special occasion. Always ask yourself, can I wear this item at least five times?
3. Search social media for people whose looks inspire you and you could see yourself having a similar

style. Start an inspiration folder and screenshot the looks that you like.

The look is important but general grooming is equally if not more important. What if you are wearing the coolest outfit but your grooming leaves a lot to be desired? As an entrepreneur, you are already busy. Why should you find the time to add another element to your job? Because as the face of your brand, being well-groomed IS your job. Book grooming appointments with yourself as if they were meetings and stick to them. Wake up an hour earlier, take advantage of the weekends, maximise your time. If you keep up your grooming schedule you will always look flawless and you'll avoid having to run around at the last minute for a wax or manicure.

Everyone has different grooming needs and standards as well as budgets. I have standing manicure and pedicure appointments during the weekends at the same local place – I don't like fancy places that cost a fortune. I get my hair cut once a quarter (as I am for ever trying to grow it) and I colour every six weeks. I love a good fake tan but could never spend the time it takes to get a decent spray tan so that's something that I do at home, usually on a Sunday evening. That way I have a good tan for the week and I can top up as needs be during the week before an event or shoot.

Updating your makeup look is easy too, from watching YouTube tutorials on how to recreate your favourite looks to going to a makeup counter, such as our Rodial counter in Harvey Nichols, which offers every customer tailor-made tutorials and advice on makeup, a concept that we rolled out to all our international stores. As I have mentioned, you should be able to recreate the look at home in just a few minutes, and that is the ethic of the Rodial counter.

In this day and age, you can keep yourself well-dressed and groomed with little investment. It is a matter of discipline. If it helps, view looking good as part of your brand rather than a luxury … it's a business expense. And yes, you can put it through your books … so get a receipt.

Overnight Success Secret #13

Ten Steps to Organise Your Wardrobe to Success

An important element of your personal branding is your image. You may question this and say, I need to be comfortable and focus on my business, this is just a waste of time. It does depend on the industry that you work in but a clean, profession-appropriate look will get you far. People judge by first impressions. Your image is a powerful asset. Whether you are pitching for new business or meeting a potential new supplier or having coffee with a blogger, you need to look the part. Getting your wardrobe in shape is the first step to looking the part.

Here are my top ten tips to managing your wardrobe for success:

1. Put the time aside to edit your wardrobe when you have a good couple of hours. Play some uplifting music and burn a candle to get in the mood.
2. Go through clothes, accessories, shoes, bags and underwear. Everything needs sorting out.
3. Put everything in three categories. LOVE: the pieces you love (obvs), wear all the time or make you feel very special when you wear them. ALTER: these are pieces that are the right look but perhaps need altering slightly because the fit isn't right before they can to be allowed back in your wardrobe. GIVE AWAY: purchases that were on the spur of

the moment and that you have no use for, pieces you haven't worn in over two years or any items that you have worn so much they are falling apart. Expensive pieces can go to online resale sites such as Vestiaire Collective, eBay or your local charity shop.

4. Buy some new hangers. I personally love the black-velvet thin hangers: they make everything look special and expensive. Sort items out by colour and by category: tops, dresses, pants, skirts. Get some lavender-scented sachets to make your closet smell good.

5. Look at your shoes and take them to the cobblers for any adjustments. I love adding a rubber sole on most of my shoes as they make them last longer and give an extra cushion of comfort.

6. Keep the clothes of the season in front view and store any out-of-season clothes in large plastic bags and put in storage. Space is important and you only want to be looking at clothes that can be worn now.

7. Try everything. Try a top with a different pair of trousers, pair of shoes, coat or accessories. Take pictures of whatever works so you can remember the look.

8. Write down a list of the gaps in your wardrobe. You don't need to buy a whole new wardrobe every season but can add a few strategic items to make your look current.

9. Search online to find the right items for you. I prefer to shop online when I am looking for something

specific as it's quicker and more efficient. I go to stores when I have more time and am looking for inspiration.

10. Go through your wardrobe four times a year and make sure it's edited, current and ready to go!

14

Stay Motivated: Coffee, Sugar and Other Stimulants

Questions I get all the time are how do I stay motivated? What gets me out of bed in the morning and keeps me going through the day? Where do I get the energy to deal with all the challenges that come my way as an entrepreneur while still having my eye on the ball?

I can't pretend it's easy, because it's not. And yes, I admit it, I can't truthfully say I am fully motivated every single hour of every single day. True, there are days that I am on cloud nine and everything is going my way, and then there are those days when I feel everything is against me and wonder why I am doing this. What if I just ran away and worked in a shoe shop? There'd be no pressure, it would all be someone else's problem ... and I could just look at shoes all day. Win, win, win. Or I could change my name and go and live on a beach in Goa making bracelets. The simple life, etc. These are the kind of thoughts that go through the mind of an average entrepreneur every day pretty much ... OK, maybe not specifically about shoes, but you get the idea. You should always be questioning your motivation and always finding the overwhelming reason to carry on. The road to success is not straightforward and neither is your journey to it. You need to find ways to keep that motivation up. Everyone can have an idea for a new business but the ones that succeed are the entrepreneurs who persevere and keep going.

For many employees, all you need to do is show up at work and your boss will be there to motivate you, coach you, encourage you or just simply annoy you. Either way, you go to work and everything sort of just happens as someone else is in charge (my shoe-shop fantasy again) and if it doesn't, well, it's no skin off your nose. As long as it wasn't your fault, you can leave it all behind and be out of the office on the dot of 5pm. And for a lot of people that's fine, I guess. If the job gets too dull and you feel you need a fresh start and a hit of new energy, you can move on, get another job with a less annoying boss and start over. But YOU (yes, I am talking directly to you now) are reading this book so you don't seem to me like that sort of person ... you are looking for something more ... you want to be challenged and you want to win. As an entrepreneur, you don't have the luxury to just show up. You have a whole team of people who are waiting for you to give them the vision, motivation and energy to make things happen for you. Unless you are there to lead your team, no one is going to do this for you. During the first few years of starting a business, it's easier to motivate yourself as you are making baby steps and every small success is really exciting. You show up and think, 'What can I do today to help my business survive another day?' In fact, pretty much every day you will find yourself in survival mode and that is a real buzz. It gives you the firepower to wake up and make things happen.

When you have been in the business for a few years and it is now a bit more stable, you have an office, a team and you get into routine. Routine is a good thing: it means that the business is running smoothly, revenues are coming in and there are no highs and lows in the business. This is a tough spot to be in for the entrepreneur. You need to find your motivation. You need to ask yourself, what drives you? Why did you get in this business in the first place? What have been the best moments since you started? Keep on telling yourself why you are doing what you are doing, find your motivation and remind yourself about it every day.

I didn't figure this out from day one. It took me a while to realise what it takes to motivate myself every single day and in return motivate my teams. The first few years in the business, I had to find a morning boost to get me going. And this was usually food related. There was a Starbucks close to my office and I would stop by religiously every morning and get an almond-cream-filled croissant with an extra-large soy cappuccino. I was having this every single day. I became addicted to it. I needed that morning sugar and caffeine hit to make me feel happy and motivated. I would arrive at the office, high on sugar, happy and super motivated for the day. I was piling on the pounds and feeling sluggish by mid-afternoon but I couldn't stop. It was working and it was the highlight of my day.

Sugar became my drug. If it wasn't the almond-cream-filled pastry, it was a hummingbird red-velvet cupcake in the afternoon or choc-chip cookie from the office kitchen. Sugar made me feel good and that made me a great leader, albeit an out-of-shape one. The more sugar I had, the more sluggish I felt and the more sugar I needed to keep going. I was officially a sugar junkie. Business was going great though, so hey, whatever works!

It took me a while to stop with the sugar addiction as my one and only motivation to drive my business. And it didn't happen overnight. The story is not too exciting but, in a nutshell, I reluctantly joined a gym, replaced my morning hit with a protein berry smoothie and got my energy boost from dry fruit and cashew nuts. I replaced the sugar-loaded soy cappuccino with organic espresso and switched to decaf after lunch. It all worked great but I wasn't getting my morning high, so how was I supposed to be motivated during the day?

Exercise first thing in the morning became my new high.

I am not going to get into the health benefits of exercise, which we all know about. But I will talk about how important exercise is for your mind and your mood when you are an entrepreneur. Nothing beats an endorphin rush you get first thing in the morning after an early workout. It really helps put you in the right frame of mind for a challenging and hectic day. Exercise works like magic to clear your mind.

There was a time when I became addicted to morning runs. If I had an issue at work, I would go through this in my mind while running and I would come up with ideas and solutions for it. I would also come up with new ideas and creative thoughts, and I would send emails straight after my morning run so my teams would be hit with these ideas as soon as they arrived at the office and could get going. I loved my morning run so much that I couldn't wait to go to bed and look forward to it, every single day. It was my creative time and my therapy. And it worked. It became a bit more challenging when the weather was cold or if it was dark in the winter and I wasn't able to run every day or as early as I wanted (I wouldn't run in the dark!) but, 8 out of 12 months a year, the outdoors was my gym and I loved it! I felt really happy and lighter and ready to face the day.

My advice would be to do something that you enjoy: it's important that you look forward to it, rather than force yourself into an activity that you don't enjoy. You might get superb abs and a pert backside (and if you do I would like to start training with you, please) but you won't get the psychological benefits ... and that's what I am most interested in. Honest. There are so many ways to exercise that we are spoilt for choice – you might love running outdoors or spinning at a studio, lifting weights at a gym or doing yoga and Pilates. There are endless exercise videos on YouTube and a number of apps that you can use to help you exercise at home if time and money are tight. And while a big endorphin-pumping workout rings my bell, you might just as easily find that head-clearing moment walking the dog or sitting on the park bench and looking at the sky ... it doesn't matter what it is ... make it part of your routine and use it to fuel your creativity and focus.

As with everything in life, you do end up getting bored doing the same thing again and again and want to change things up a bit. My focus now is on training at the gym. I discovered yoga, and while it would never be my full-on choice of exercise (I needed to burn those calories and get those cardio sessions into my schedule) I did find that it was great to lengthen the muscles and get a great stretch and also clear my mind. So, if I had a major issue at work, yoga was great to really calm me down and get me to see a new perspective. I never regularly practised yoga but at times of stress I would increase my yoga sessions and that seemed to work.

You may ask yourself, 'Where will I find the time to meditate or exercise? I barely have enough time to run my life and my business as it is.' I am a big believer in setting my alarm an hour earlier than usual and fitting it all in. My alarm is set for 5.50am every day. I take 10–25 minutes to meditate and set my intention for the day, then I walk to my local gym where I start a class by 7.15. It is important for me to go to the gym first thing before I start coming up with excuses why I shouldn't exercise, and you should watch out for that ... I found it too easy to come up with a reason not go when I trained at lunchtimes or after work. But if you really can't do early mornings then make sure you commit the time. Exercise is booked in to my schedule the way meetings are so I just follow my schedule. Am I super-motivated to exercise every day? Not really. But I do it ... consistency is important. Even if I don't feel like it, I still show up. Some days I give it 100 per cent, some days I only manage about 50 per cent ... either way I still come out feeling amazing. And that's what keeps me coming back.

I discovered meditation a couple of years ago. I was aware of it but always thought this was something for the Buddhists or bohemian crowd who do yoga all day and don't have real jobs. Maybe this was the case 30 years ago, but I discovered that meditation has really evolved and become a lot more Westernised through a number of apps and websites, and its principles can be applied to the modern-day life to keep us grounded and focused. I subscribed to an app called Headspace that has all sorts of meditations with themes ranging from how to get you focused to how to be creative or deal with negative emotions. You don't just sit down breathing by yourself: there is someone guiding you through what you should be thinking (or not thinking) and almost manipulating you into a state of feeling calm and collected. You can sit down for as little as ten minutes in the morning and that's all you need to do. I love meditating first thing as it helps me set the tone for the day. But sometimes, when things are getting particularly hectic, I have found myself meditating in cars and planes: I just put my on headphones and a pair of oversized sunglasses, I play a ten-minute meditation on the app, and I'm good to go.

What can meditation do for you?

1. It will help you deal with difficult situations. As an entrepreneur, you will always be faced

with challenges and nine times out of ten the issues are with people. There can be a conflict with someone in your business, whether it's staff, a supplier or someone with whom you are collaborating. By meditating, you will find that you deal with everything in a calm and collected manner, as if you are advising a third person. Since I started meditating, I have found that I am not taking things personally (at least most times) and try to see the other person's point of view. Meditation teaches you that it's not about winning an argument, it's about resolving a situation in the calmest possible way. And that means you feel good about yourself.

2. It will make you be in control (or look like you are). Again, in times of crisis, your team needs to know that you are in charge, that you are dealing with whatever challenges your company is going through. Things will never be perfect, but if you are calm and collected you will be in control, and this is a sign of a good leader. People will respect you for this and follow your leadership.

3. Remind yourself why you are doing what you are doing. Sometimes we get lost and forget our goals. Meditation helps set your intentions for the day, week, month and year ahead of you. You take a few minutes out of your day to breathe and remind yourself why you started this business in the first place and what it is that keeps you going. Your initial motivation doesn't change but sometimes we get surrounded by so much noise that we get confused and disorientated ... we forget what makes us happy. A few minutes at the beginning of your day is all you need to

reacquaint yourself with your motivation, remind yourself of your happy place and set out your goals for the day, no matter how small. This technique certainly works for me and helps me to keep that essential motivation, day in, day out.

Overnight Success Secret #14

Coping with Stress

As an entrepreneur and subsequently the queen (or king) of your own castle, everyone wants a piece of you. Your staff, your customers, your suppliers, your family. There are times that it feels like there are not enough hours in the day to get everything done. Time is your enemy. You always seem to be running out of time and you are faced with problems coming from all different directions. Then you reach a point where we feel overwhelmed and ready to explode. Your stress levels rise, which can lead to mental or physical breakdown. You start feeling unwell; your skin and hair looks bad; you may gain weight, resorting to comfort food and drink that may momentarily give you a boost but doesn't make you feel good in the long run. You tend to go for quick fixes, which is exactly what these are. Quick and fixes. Not long-term solutions for dealing with stress.

How can you get it all done without having a meltdown? When your life becomes all about prioritising others, you need to find those moments to connect with yourself, reset and rebalance. You need the time to centre yourself. You need to find a mechanism to rebalance. Find a way to mindfully focus on what you are doing at the moment and stop worrying about what is going to happen in the future and when you will tackle your to-do lists. Dealing with stress is a very personal thing but it can only happen if you are committed to making changes.

Here you go: five steps to help you cope with stress.

1. Nourish your body. Being a modern person, you probably know everything there is to know about healthy eating, from your Atkins to your South Beach diet, from your quinoa to your gluten frees. I am not going to preach to you about how you should eat healthily or count your calories ... I am asking you to treat food as fuel that will help your body deal with stress. The same way we use antioxidant ingredients in skincare to fight against free radicals, we need to eat antioxidant-packed food to help us deal with stress.

    It goes without saying that fruit and vegetables, grains and lean protein are great for you. If you feel lethargic, low energy and very stressed, reach out for a green juice or smoothie rather than a soft drink and muffin. They might give you instant satisfaction but they make you feel worse.

    Also, a word on fad diets. They can drain your immune system and make you sick – you will probably return to your old junk-food routine and put any weight back on. And counting calories, that's wrong too. You can't deprive your body of essential fuel: if you are hungry, you are hungry, you can't trick your body. Embrace good fat sources, from nuts to oily fish, as they are not just great at making you feel full but also nourish your body too. And have protein with every meal to make you feel full for longer and help build lean muscle.

2. Strategise your to-do list. Lists are your best friend. I find nothing more satisfying than starting a list of

things to do, crossing out every task and then having a fully crossed-out page at the end of the day. Get the most cumbersome tasks done early in the morning and early in the week (first thing Monday morning is the best time) when your head is clear and your willpower is at its highest point. Once you get the smaller, annoying things done, then you can move on to more strategic things that you enjoy doing.

It's a small detail, but I always like to have beautiful notepads and coloured pens that make list making a bit more fun.

3. Rest. No one can work 24/7 and still be productive and creative. Rest is as important as moving and working. Rest helps the body recover from stress. Ideally, rest would mean sitting in stillness where you can relax body and mind. Watching TV and browsing the internet or checking social media are not ideal, as your mind is still active and thinking. But I do have to admit that sometimes after a stressful day I don't really mind watching my favourite series or checking on what I missed on social media during the day.

Sleep is equally important. Try to go to bed an hour earlier as your body gets into the REM state quicker the earlier you go to bed. You need your sleep to feel rested and full of energy the next day. Lack of sleep can make you cranky, unfocused and will make you reach out for junk food. So get as much sleep as you can during the week and lie in a little during the weekend.

4. Be social. And by social I don't mean spend endless hours on Facebook. I mean cultivate

those relationships that lift you and get rid of any toxic ones. Find the people with the right energy and spend time with them, meet with them, pick up the phone and have a chat. Step back from any relationships with friends or family that were based on things you had in common in the past and you don't any more. And people who bring you down or drain you: clear them out of your life. Healthy relationships help reduce stress, put things in perspective and make you happier.

5. Reconnect with nature. Any opportunity you have, spend some time in nature. A walk in the park, by a lake or the sea. I try to have a walk in the park every weekend. It helps me clear my head and decongest from any stressful situations that I was involved with over the week. I sometimes come up with new ideas or solutions to problems when I walk, although I am not looking for them! You don't want your relaxing walk to have the stress of coming up with solutions to problems, as all you will be thinking about during the walk will be the problem itself! Take your dog for a walk, or get a dog (!). Nature brings a natural state of relaxation. If you can combine this with a tech switch off, this is a double whammy! This is easier said than done but do try once a week to take some time away from your phone, social media and anything tech.

As exercise is an important part of my life, I want to share with you some of my tips for keeping up with exercise:

1. Invest in some workout clothes that make you feel great. If you put your old sweats and old T-shirt on, you won't feel that great. It's all about feeling good about yourself when you exercise – it will keep you motivated for longer. I like to add a couple of new pieces every quarter to update my workout wardrobe and give away anything that has seen better days. If I look good, I feel good and I know I will be a lot more motivated for my workout.

2. Try different gyms and classes until you find what you like. There are apps such as Mind Body that show you the gyms around your area. Explore new workout types and keep things fresh. Your body gets used to a certain routine and after you've been doing the same thing for a while you stop seeing changes. Also, try to mix it up. We should all be doing cardio to keep us healthy and fit, resistance work with weights/elastic bands or TRX for keeping our muscles conditioned and stretch to avoid injury. This is a lot but there are many classes out there that offer all three elements together. You just need to do your research.

3. Stick to a gym that is close to you. Convenience is really important for consistency. If the gym is more than ten minutes away by transport, it may not last for long. I always find a gym close to home so I can walk, and thankfully there are gyms everywhere these days. On the days that I am not motivated at all to workout (and yes, it happens really often!) I just put on my favourite workout outfit, walk to the gym (still unmotivated), and when I am in the class with great music and a motivational instructor,

I get through it. At least I show up, and keeping consistency is more important than waiting for that day that you are fully motivated.

4. Don't commit to expensive memberships. Find places that get you to pay per class, so you can be flexible and move around if you need to keep things fresh. Thankfully the gym business has really changed over the last few years. We have all experienced paying an expensive joining fee plus monthly charges for a gym we hardly ever went to. Not only that but the contracts were locked in for a year at a time and you couldn't get out of it. One of the reasons I didn't exercise in the past was that I was so resentful of those sneaky gym contracts that I couldn't face those gyms any more. They weren't gyms, they were money traps. Thank God things have changed and there are some amazing gyms out there that you can pay per class. Not only that but there are online apps such as Mind body through which you can book a class from a selection of gyms in your area with a click of a button.

5. Exercise first thing in the morning when your willpower is at its highest. Wouldn't it be great to get yourself to the gym early on before you realised what you were doing and before you started using all sorts of excuses not to go? Plan it in your diary like a meeting. Workout, then shower, get dressed and go off to work. You're all done and you don't have to think about this for the rest of the day. On top of this, you will feel amazing and a lot more productive and positive for your day ahead. If you are an evening person and you'd rather workout

later, that can work too, as long as you keep it consistent.

6. I am not sure that this is medically advisable, but I have a shot of espresso before I exercise. I find this gives me the energy that I need for a good workout, especially since I just jump out of bed and then off to the gym. I need something to give me the energy and motivation, and camomile tea just won't cut it. Again, think about how to get yourself into a state of mind to exercise. It may be a drink ritual or having your workout clothes ready to go (I have heard cases of people who actually wear their workout clothes in bed so they are ready to go first thing, but that would be overkill . . .). Or it may be a glass of freshly squeezed orange juice or a protein smoothie: whatever works to give you the energy that you need.

7. Share your workout plans on social media. This way it makes you commit to them and you get the encouragement of your friends and followers. Once you commit and tell your friends about your plans, you almost make a promise to them that you will keep. Sometimes we are better at keeping our promises to our friends than ourselves. And every time you post a picture of your workout and get your friends to like it, it's as if you are getting their seal of approval. Well, that's a great motivator to keep you going, right?

8. Keep your playlists current. I tend to workout better when the music motivates me. If the music is out of beat or old fashioned or I am listening to the same playlist again and again, I can't

get motivated. I've had spinning classes where I gave it 100 per cent with the right music and others where all I could think of was when will this torture of a playlist end, and needless to say I didn't work out nearly as hard. How do you keep your playlists current? Subscribe to Spotify, which gives you lots of workout lists from gyms and others so you always have fresh music to keep you motivated.

9. Reward yourself. There are all types of rewards that you may enjoy. It could be a cheat food day of the week, as the gym addicts call the day that they can have anything unhealthy (including burger, pizza, pasta, fries, ice cream – hopefully not all at the same time). Or it could be a new pair of jeans to celebrate your new shape or a sneaky ab selfie to post on Instagram. New workout clothes always work and take you back to that motivation element. Reward yourself in the way that makes you feel happy. You've taken time out of your day, you've worked hard, you deserve it!

10. Be consistent. Success in business, as we have seen, is all about doing small things consistently and keeping up with your efforts. The same goes for exercise. You need consistency to see results. Once you start skipping a day here, a day there, you will stop working out altogether. Keep it up even if it means you don't give it all some days: just show up, go through with it and that sets the tone for a better workout the next day. Consistency is key.

15

Make it Happen

When I moved into my first office, having worked from home for a few years, the business felt real, Rodial felt real. In the early years of the business, when all that was driving me and my team was sheer passion and nothing else, we always said to each other the same phrase when facing a challenge: 'Make it happen.' And we always did. I had this phrase mounted and placed on the wall in my office and, with every move, that phrase comes with me. The team knows it, the suppliers know it, and new visitors know it. We all hashtag it on Twitter and Instagram and it's our not-very-secret code.

I set up the business against all odds, when investors didn't believe in it (or me), buyers didn't answer my calls, friends doubted me. This is the number one lesson in entrepreneurism: you have to believe in yourself even if no one else will.

I wasn't the prettiest or the smartest girl at school. I completed my studies but just about got through. I never got my first choice of a company or job and I got fired. I never had a plan to be an entrepreneur and I got into it out of lack of other options. But I persevered. Over the years, I have seen beauty brands come and go, the founders giving up after a few years when the going gets tough.

To recap, if your plan is to get rich quick, being an entrepreneur won't get you where you want to be. I didn't get a salary for the first five years and when I did I was paid less than the receptionist. I was putting the money back into the business. Don't be an entrepreneur if you want to work little and lead a leisurely lifestyle. Since I started the business I have been working evenings, early mornings and weekends. This is my passion and my own company so I never think about it as work but it's not a holiday either. And talking about holidays. forget extended breaks. Anything more than a week away from work makes me nervous and I can never switch off. When you have your own business, you need to deal with problems – and they won't go away when you are on holiday.

On the flip side, having my own business that is my passion makes me truly happy. I can be creative and drive the business in all different directions and this energises me. I work with very smart and ambitious people and that is a great motivator.

I wouldn't have my life any other way. You have to get into this for the right reasons. Because you love it, you are passionate for it and you are resilient and hardworking enough to get through any hardships. Passion won't protect you from hardship, but it ensures you will keep going ... or, in other words, you will pick yourself up, dust yourself off and start over.

If you are an entrepreneur, the world is entirely yours to discover and create. A lot of people will try to discourage you and give you the wrong advice – 'it's a competitive industry, you can't do it alone, a lot of people failed, you'll lose money, you'll waste your time' – you can't listen to any of this.

But how can you always believe in yourself? With all of us there are moments of hesitation. Am I doing the right thing? Will I ever be successful? When will my business take off?

There are struggles daily and you will find a lot of reasons to give up.

Being an entrepreneur is hard work. You'll receive all the rejections that you can imagine and you'll have to keep going. It will take longer to achieve your dreams than you think. Nothing will happen easily. Anything that can go wrong will go wrong. I had no idea at the beginning how difficult it would be. But then you have those small victories, those moments when something amazing happens for you and your business, and that keeps you going. At the hardest moments through my journey, I sometimes take a step back and remind myself why I am doing what I am doing. And it makes it all worth it.

And make sure you are always grounded and get the support that you need from those close to you. I am eternally grateful to my husband, young boys and family who surround me with their love and support, and I couldn't be who I am without them. A stable family life is really important for success. As your mind is on the business 24/7, your family will hopefully understand, support you and be there for you along your journey. The days when I had coffee with girlfriends and was hosting impromptu dinners at home were over when I started my business. You have to make sacrifices as time is limited and I made the decision very early on that I need to focus on my family, my team and work – and sadly everything else has to give.

But I don't feel bad in any way that I don't have a booming social calendar outside work as this isn't something that is important for me. I love spending all my work time with my team and business associates and all my other time with my family – that is exactly what makes me happy. As everything in life is about prioritising what is important to you, especially when you have your own business, you need to be very clear about your priorities and stick to them.

I hope you enjoyed reading about my story and hope I inspired you to pursue your own overnight success.

The road will be bumpy and there will be challenges, but if you love what you do and you have a real passion for it you are already close to being an overnight success.

My Top Five Tips to Success

1. My first tip is to find your motivation. Everyone (including myself) needs to be motivated day to day. It can be hard. I can't say I wake up every day feeling super motivated ... it takes time and it takes a lot of hard work. So how do you motivate yourself? Identify the people that you admire and follow them on social media. Go on YouTube and watch motivational clips, attend conferences and listen to people making motivational speeches. Follow people who you think have done really well in their careers and find out how they did it. In this day and age, there is so much information about motivational figures out there, so find out who they are and what steps they took. If you listen to their tips and read a bit more about their journey, you can pick up some handy lessons along the way. I also find reading books is a great way to get motivated. I love reading books about women who started from nothing and have grown to be the most amazing businesswomen and public figures. My favourite books are *#Girlboss* by Sophia Amoruso and *Leave Your Mark* by Aliza Licht. I really enjoyed reading about their journeys and the challenges they had. So, read, educate yourself and watch a lot of motivational videos.
2. Don't be afraid to ask for advice. I feel this is a really important point. It doesn't matter how long you have been in an industry or how successful

you are – asking for other people's opinions is a positive thing. It is not a weakness and doesn't mean you don't know what you are doing. Sometimes it is helpful to get another person's point of view on a situation. Even if it's having a chat with your group of girlfriends over a coffee or organising a meeting with colleagues to discuss an idea, people on the outside of a situation looking in may make points and highlight things that you have not noticed yourself. Asking questions and taking in different angles/points of view on a situation is a good skill to have and you can build even better ideas. You need to build up your knowledge as you can't be an expert on absolutely everything, so asking for advice, particularly from industry experts, can come in very handy.

3. It's very important to believe in yourself. This may seem like an obvious tip but it is one that is underestimated. If you don't believe in yourself, no one else will! You must be your own biggest supporter in all areas of life in order to achieve everything you wish. Focus on your strengths rather than your weaknesses – obviously, it's good to be aware of your weaknesses but you need to ensure you don't make these your focal point otherwise they can undermine your confidence in yourself! Another important lesson to learn is to not compare yourself to others. This can be tricky as it is human nature to make comparisons. But remember, no matter how successful/beautiful/ smart people may seem, every single person has

insecurities. Don't compare yourself to others as you are unique and have something that no one else can offer.

4. My fourth tip is to always keep learning. If you keep doing the exact same thing you have been doing for the past few years you will get the exact same results. You need to challenge yourself and learn new skills. Keep a close eye on new developments in every industry. Go and attend a seminar, take a course or do something online. There are so many ways now that you can keep yourself learning and keep yourself ahead of the game – you can't do the same thing again and again and expect to be successful. It's all about finding out what the new trends are: if you are working in fashion/beauty you need to be watching YouTube tutorials and looking at what the new trends coming up will be. It's all about learning and challenging yourself so that you can be the best you can be. You will find that the most successful people in the world never say, 'Oh I am so successful, this is it.' They reinvent themselves. It's all about learning and progressing.

5. Always look your best. I find that when I look and feel my best I am far more productive and come up with better ideas. Identify the clothes that make you feel good and confident and keep them in a corner of your closet so that you can easily access them. I'm not saying you have to go shopping for a whole new wardrobe, but knowing what outfits and makeup make you feel your best can

give you that extra added confidence boost
and help you stay motivated. It also means that
when you're meeting with new potential clients or
partners you are putting forward the best version
of yourself, and it's always good to make a strong
impression.

Join the Overnight Success Community

You can't keep up your drive and inspiration alone. You need to be surrounded by a community of like-minded people who support and encourage you. I myself look for inspiration and motivation every day from successful women around me, reading books, checking out blogs and attending conferences. Inspiration is a living organism and we need to feed it every day. I want you to have that ongoing inspiration too.

Here is a short list of free but helpful resources you can access to keep your inspiration alive:

For business ideas: Entrepreneur.com, Inc.com, Thestartupmag.com
For a business angles on beauty and fashion brands: fashionweekdaily.com, wwd.com, bof.com
For fashion inspiration: Pinterest and Instagram

Check out my website

www.mariahatzistefanis.com for my blog and info on my next speaking engagements where I aim to empower and motivate. Also, check out our websites www.rodial.co.uk

and www.nipandfab.com to find out more about the products mentioned in the book.

Connect with me on social media

Connect with me on Instagram and Twitter @mrsrodial for feedback, questions and my regular motivational quotes. Use the hashtags #mrsrodial and #overnightsuccess

Acknowledgements

I'd like to thank my editors at Ebury, Carey Smith and Lydia Good for believing in my book after only seeing a half finished version of it. They gave me the kick in the butt I needed to get it finished. I am grateful for the opportunity after I'd been rejected by three other publishers – there's nothing like an overnight success in book publishing either. My husband, Stratis, for taking me seriously about writing a book even when no one else did. A huge thank you to Sean Cunning for helping me to edit the book and for teaching me to keep things light. My illustrator Emma Kenny for drawing the most fabulous illustration for my book cover and for bearing with me with those 1am emails when I would wake up panicked about whether we should go with pants or a skirt. We got there at the end. Finally, I'd love to thank my teams at Rodial and Nip+Fab, our loyal customers and our amazing retailers who inspire me every single day.

INDEX

In *Thrive*, Arianna Huffington, the co-founder and editor-in-chief of the *Huffington Post* and one of the most influential women in the world, has written a passionate call to arms, looking to redefine what it means to be successful in today's world.

She likens our drive for money and power to two legs of a three-legged stool. It may hold us up temporarily, but sooner or later we're going to topple over. We need a third leg – a Third Metric for defining success – in order to live a healthy, productive, and meaningful life.

In this deeply personal book, Arianna talks candidly about her own challenges with managing time and prioritising the demands of a career and two daughters. Drawing on the latest ground-breaking research and scientific findings in the fields of psychology, sports, sleep and physiology that show the profound and transformative effects of meditation, mindfulness, unplugging and giving, Arianna shows us the way to a revolution in our culture, our thinking, our workplaces, and our lives.